Adorable Town

✓ **45** adorable **coloring** pages 📓
✓ **Great for aspiring** adults **and** teens 😊
✓ **Ideal for** colored **pencils, markers or colored pencils** ✏️
✓ Large **print page** format: **8.5 x 11 inches** 📕
✓ **Single-sided** pages **to avoid spills, ensuring your masterpieces stay clean** ✒️
✓ Activity **to help** artists **relax and explore creativity** ♥
✓ **Reduces anxiety** ★

Copyright © 2024 by Al&Vy

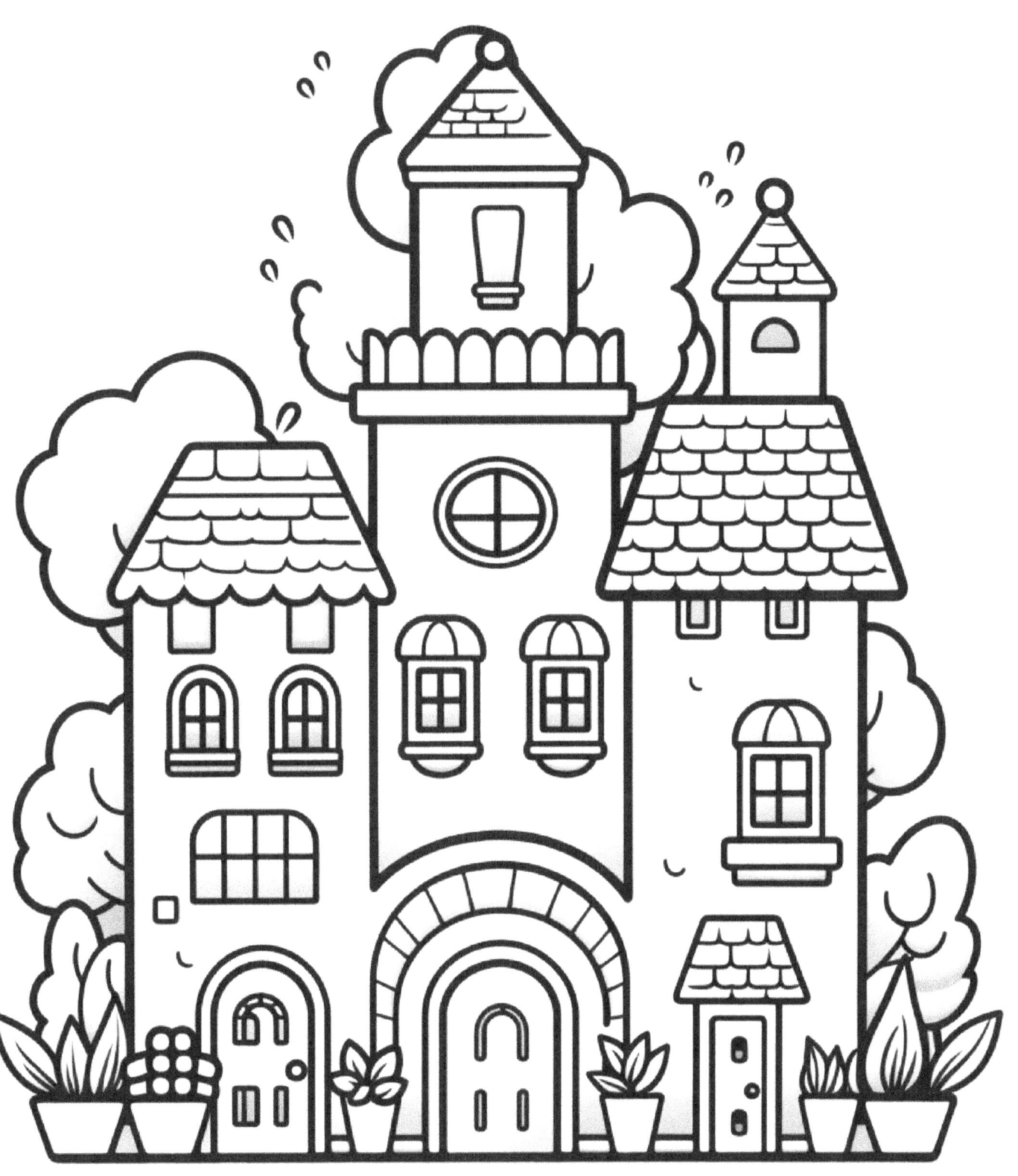

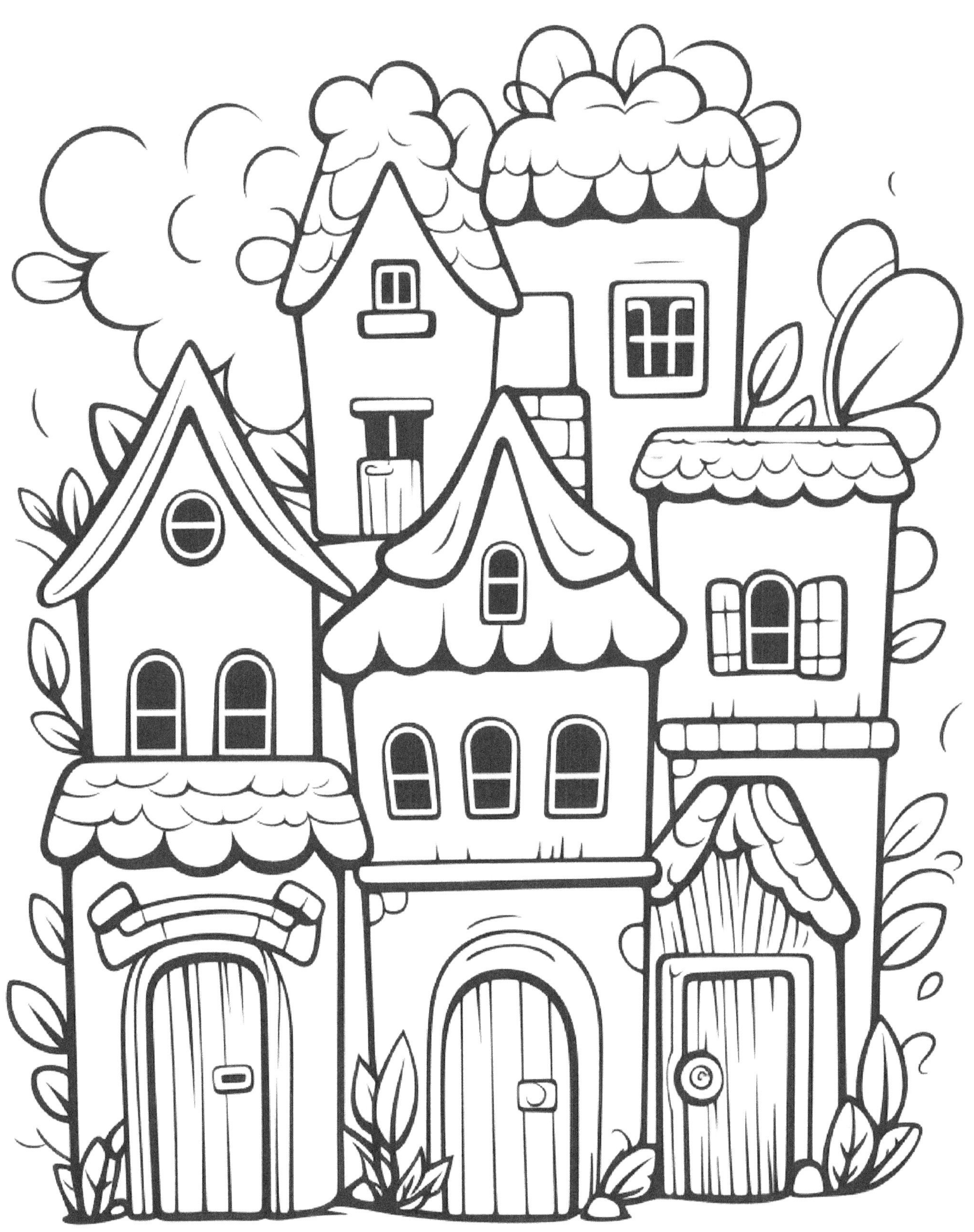

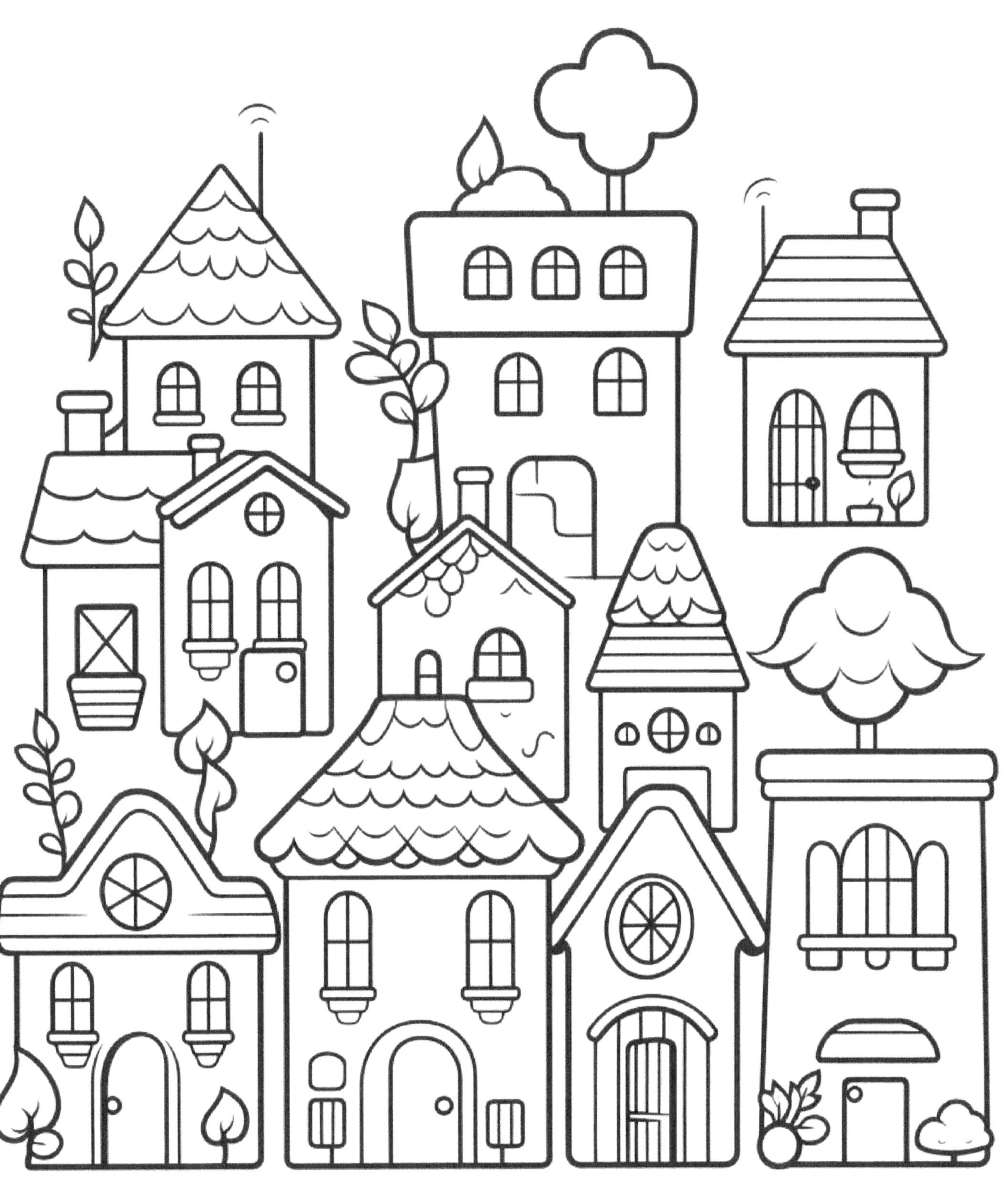

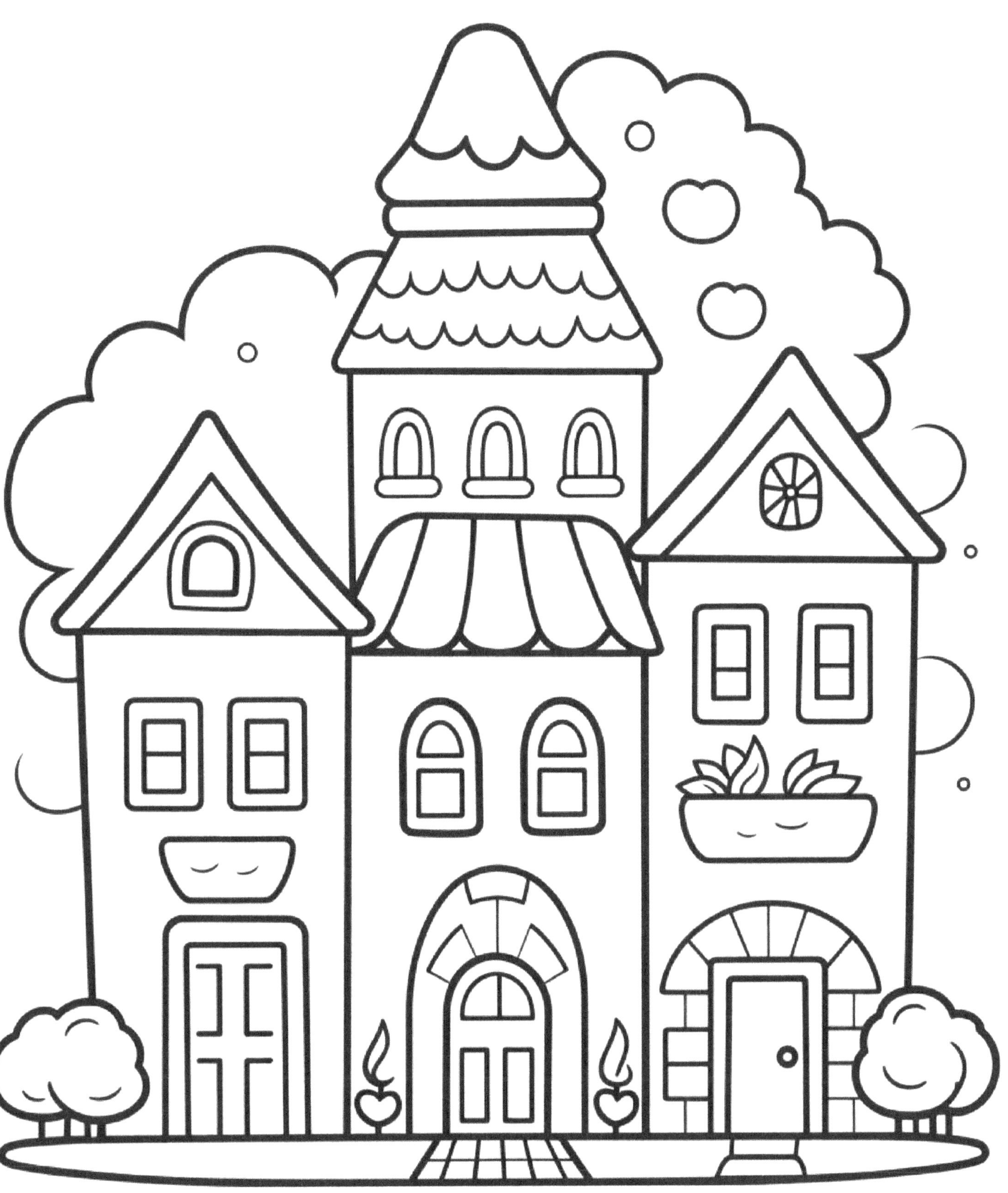

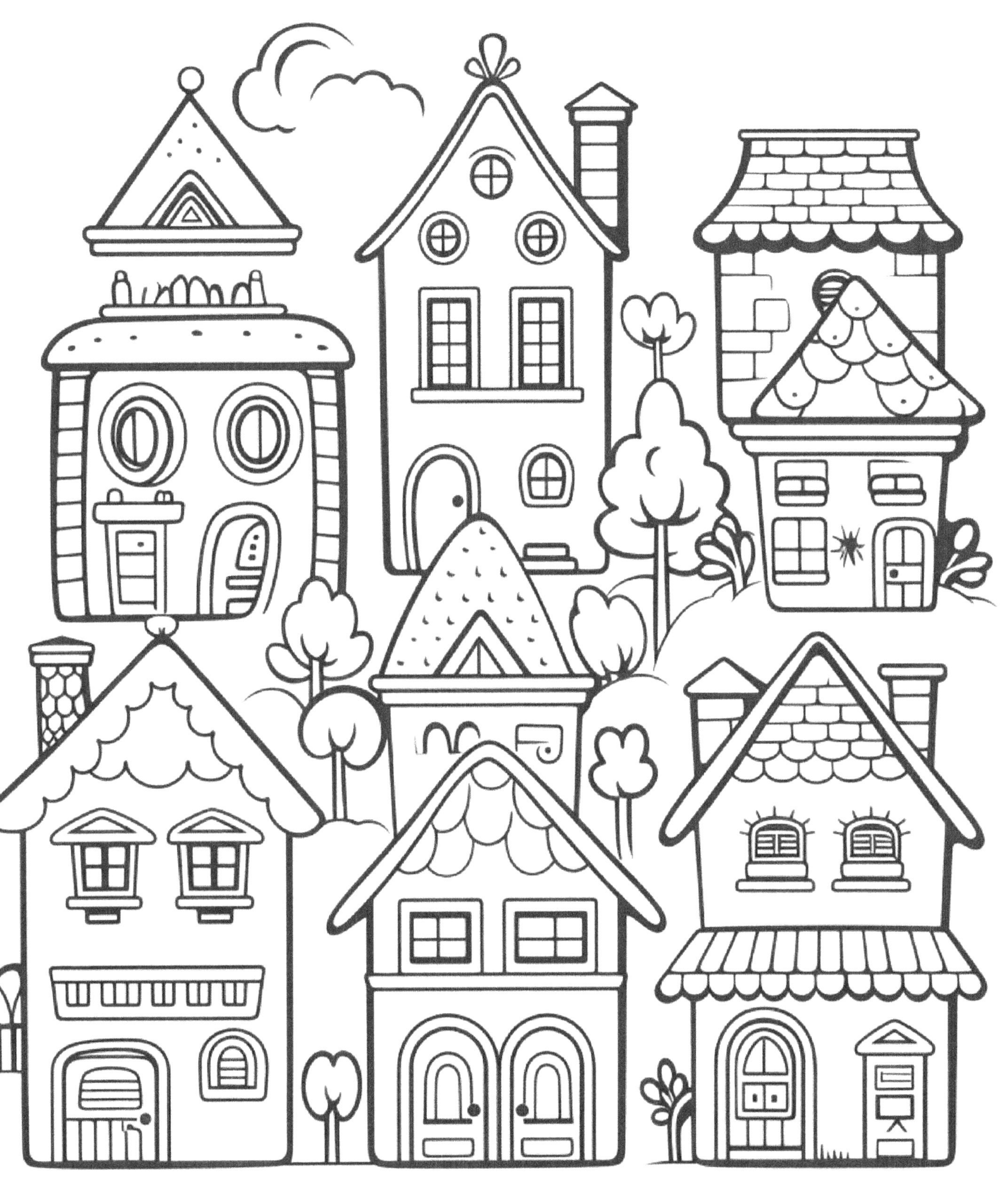

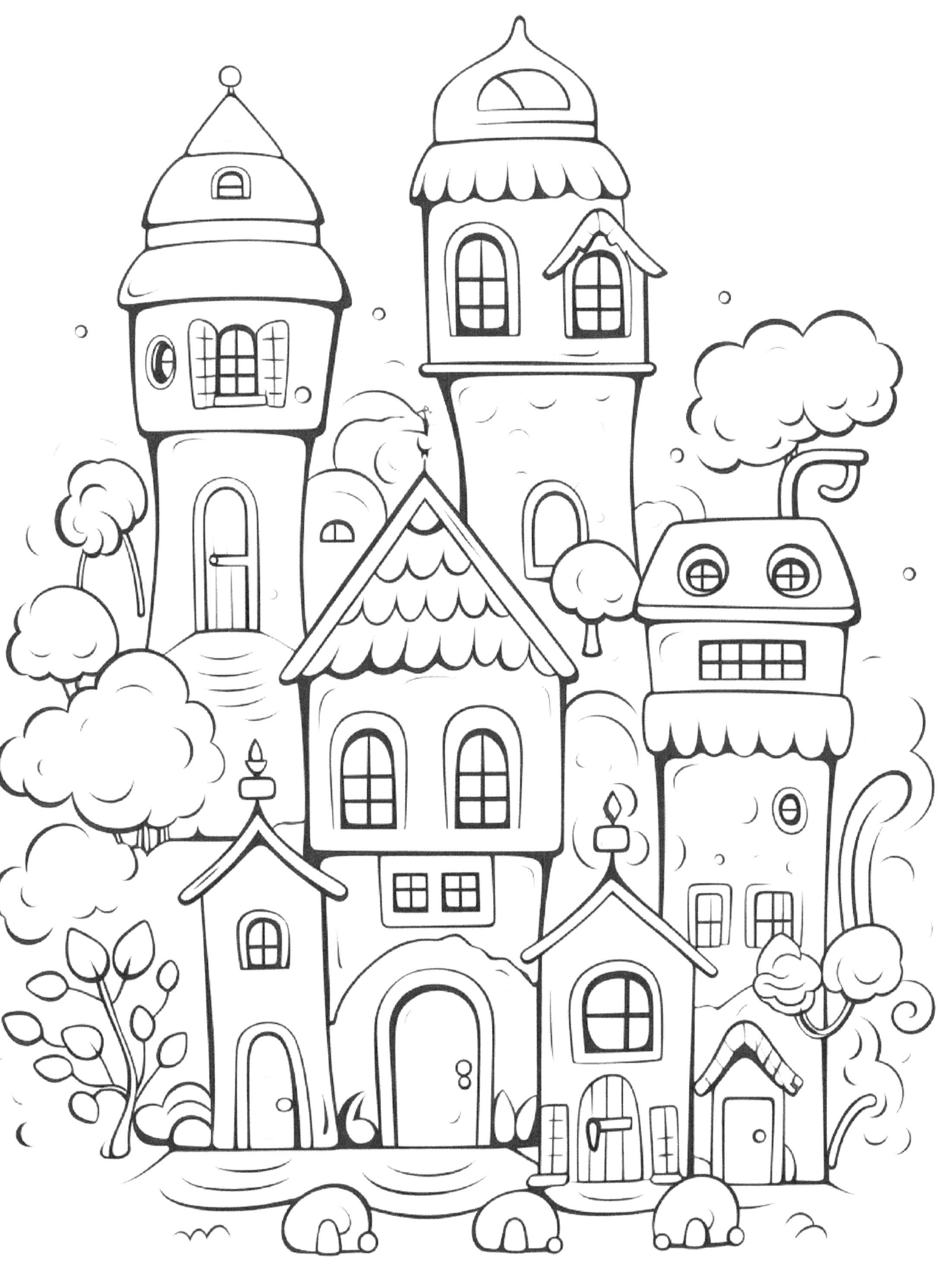

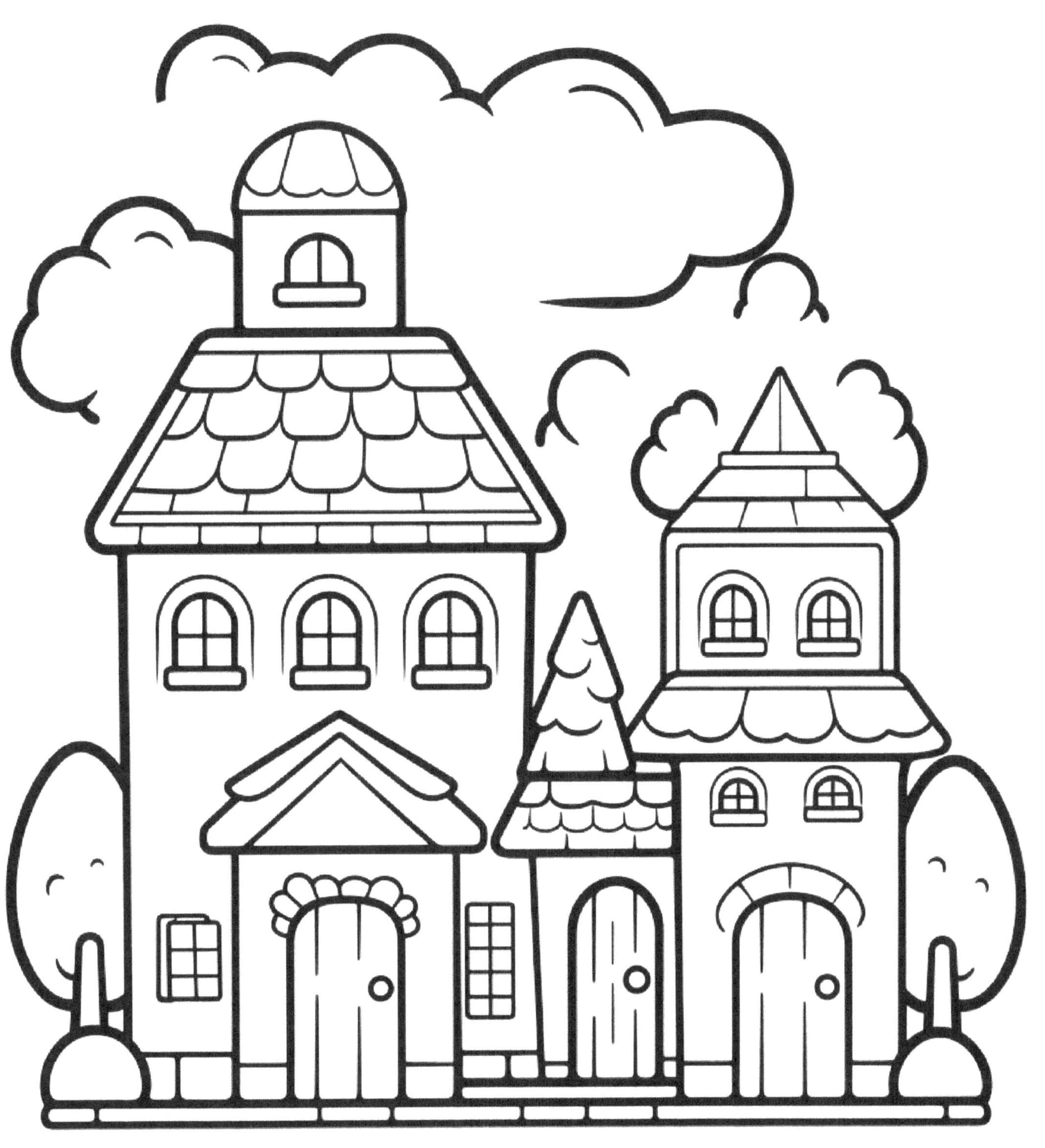

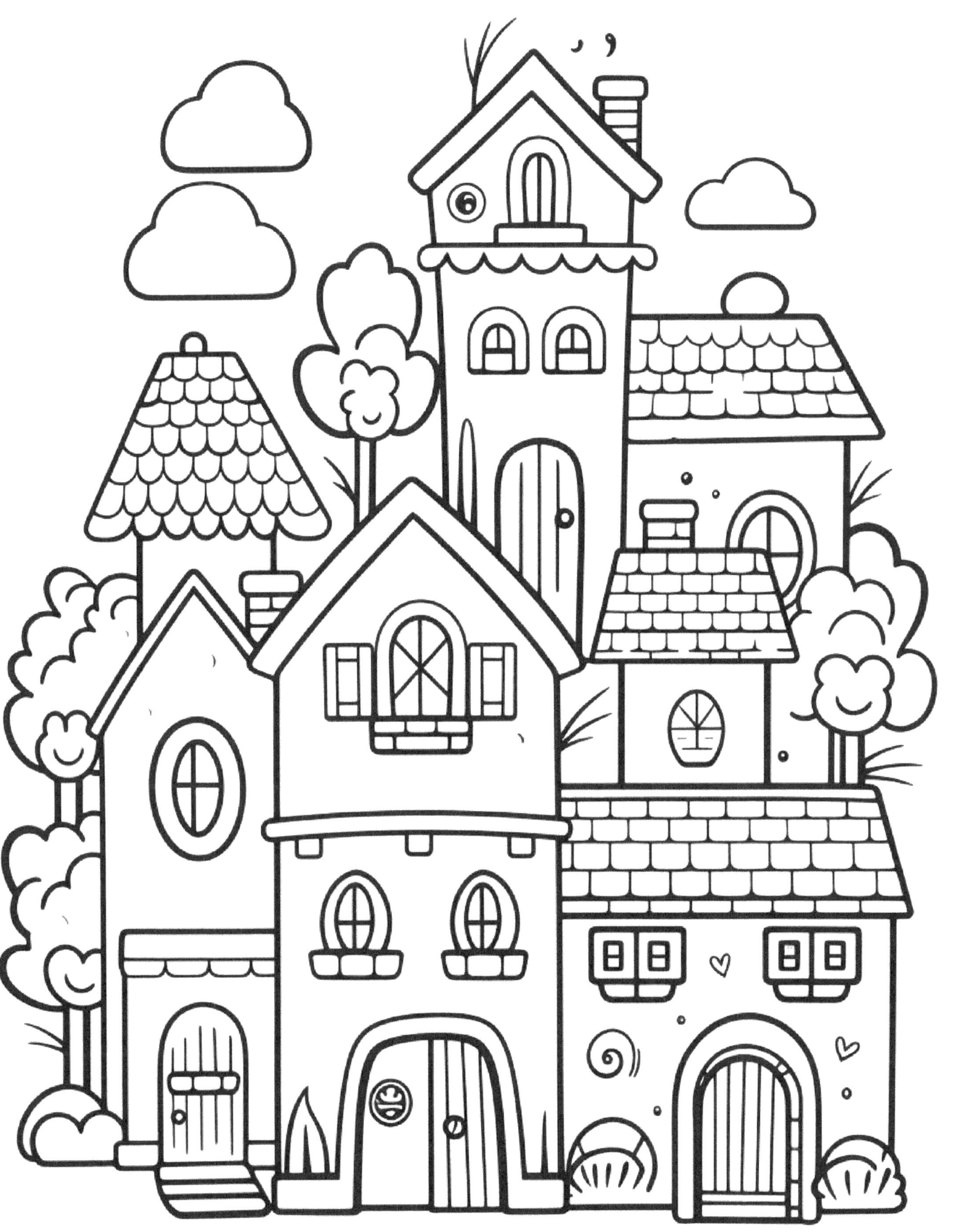

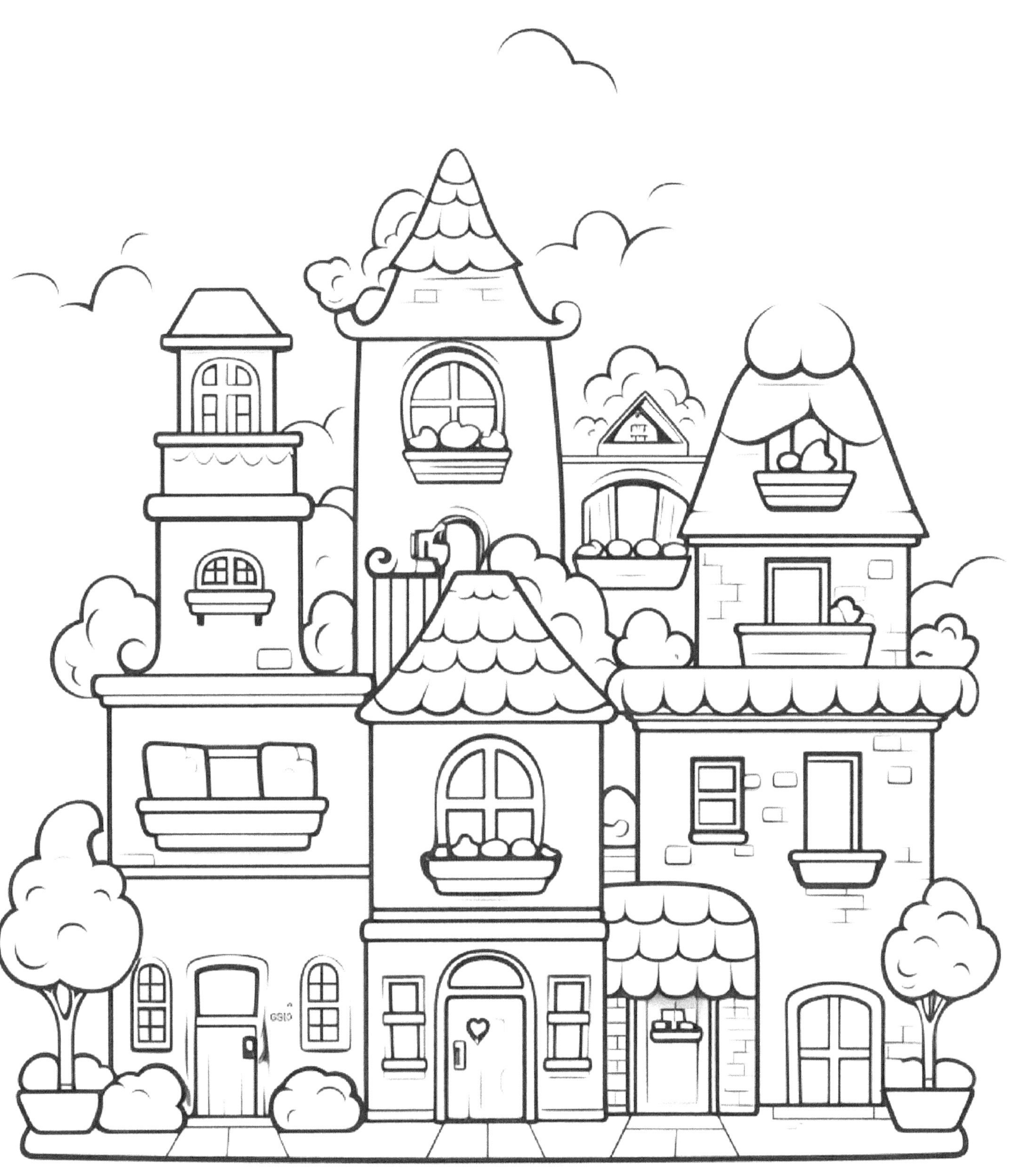

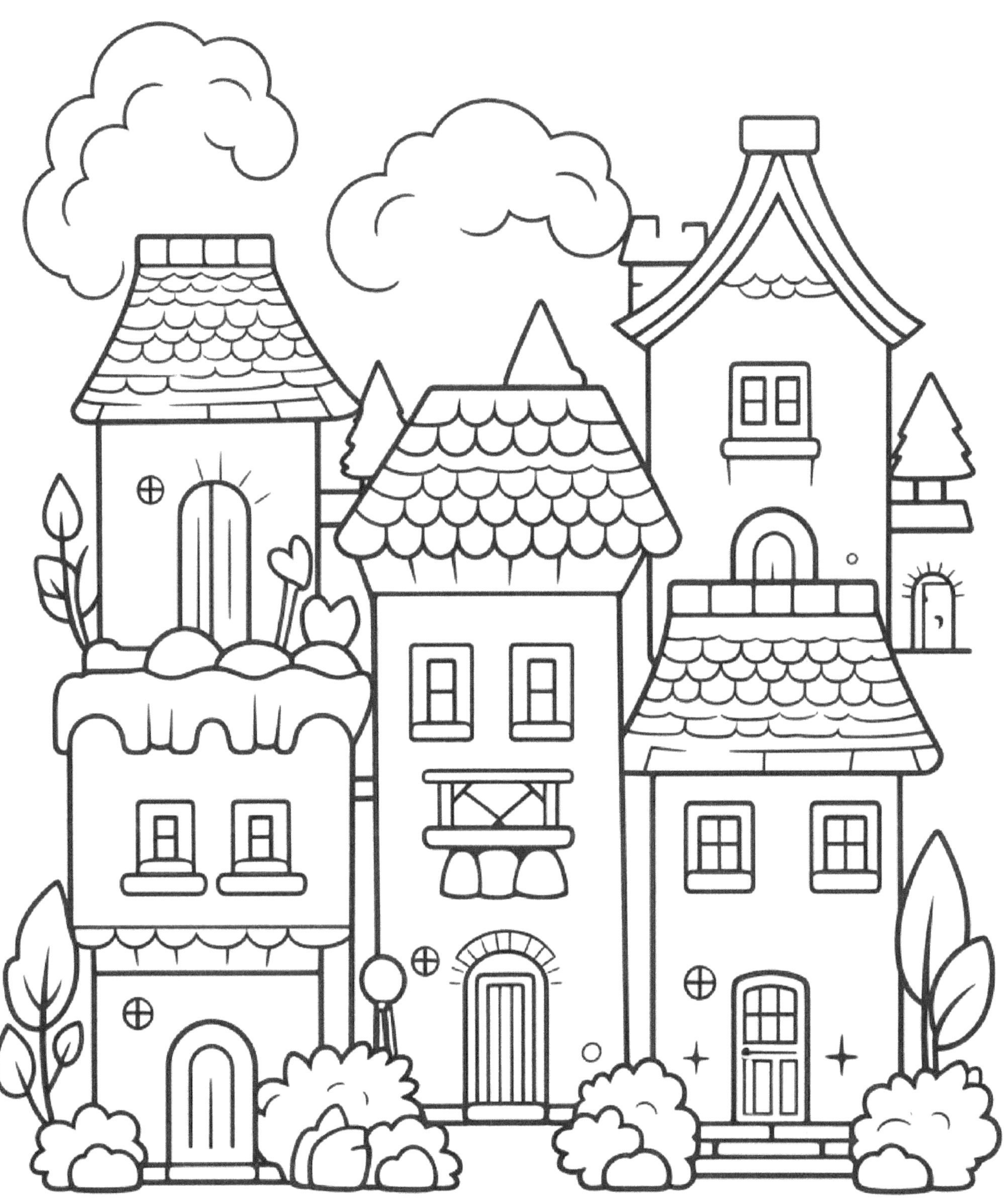

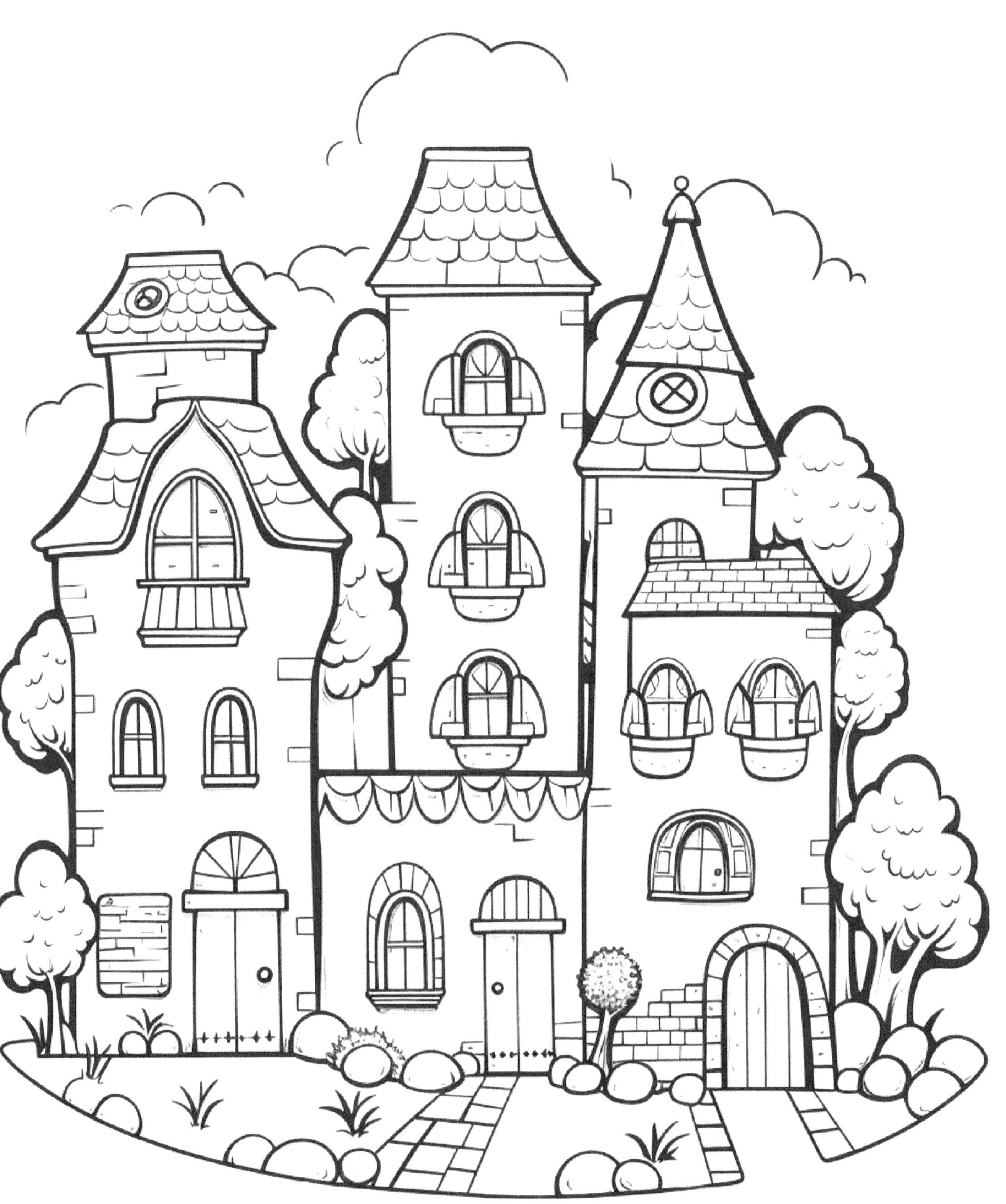

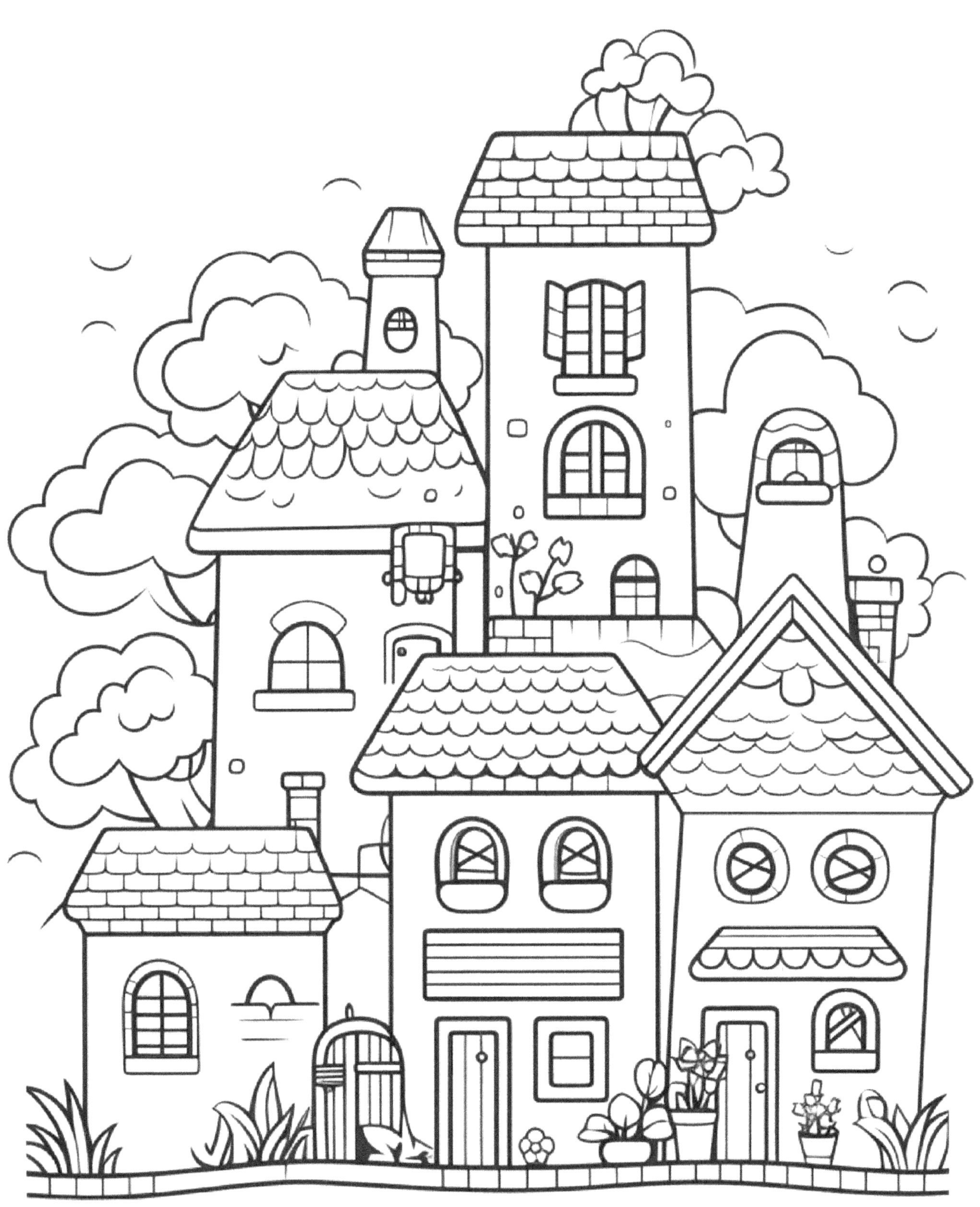

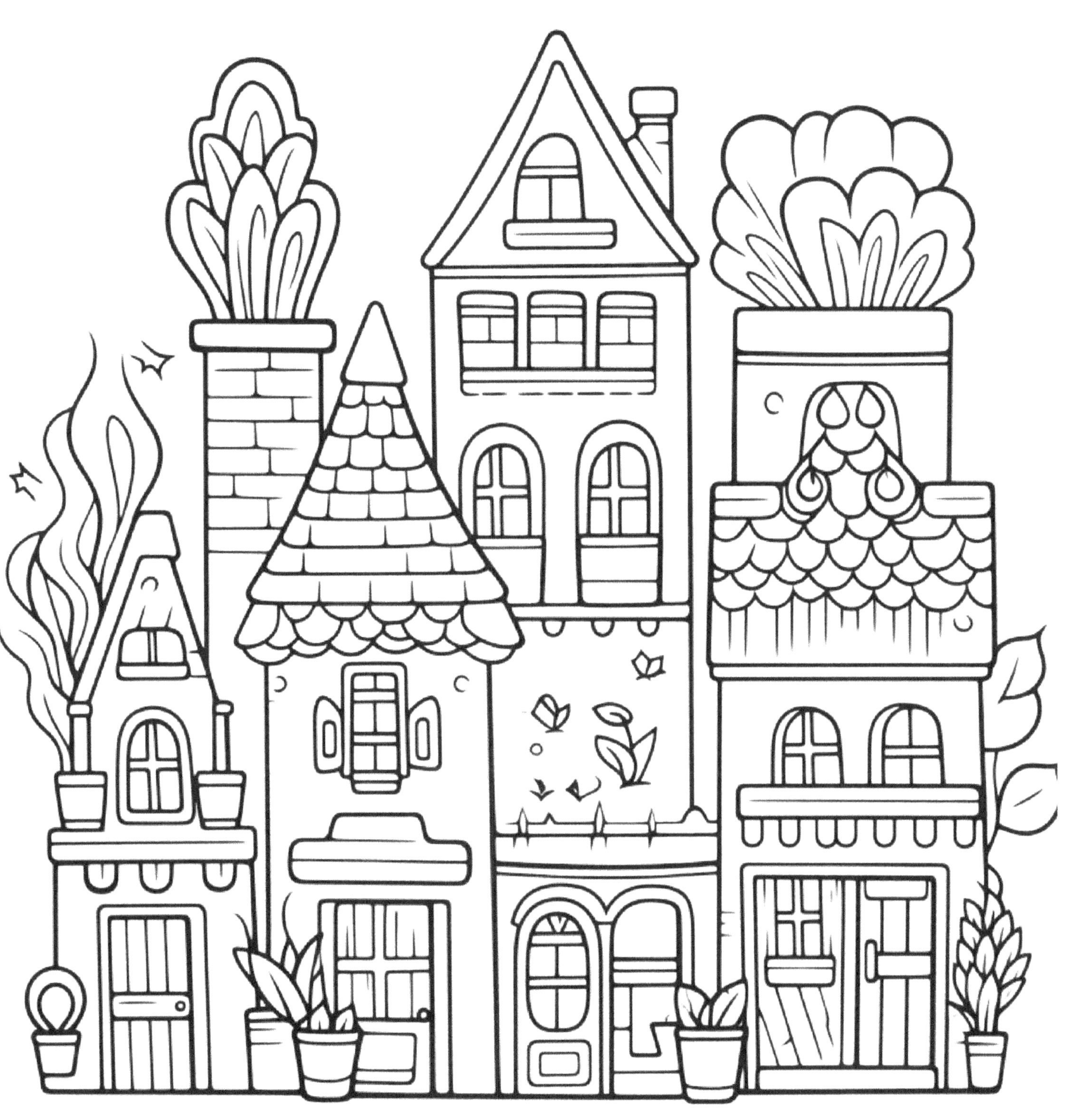

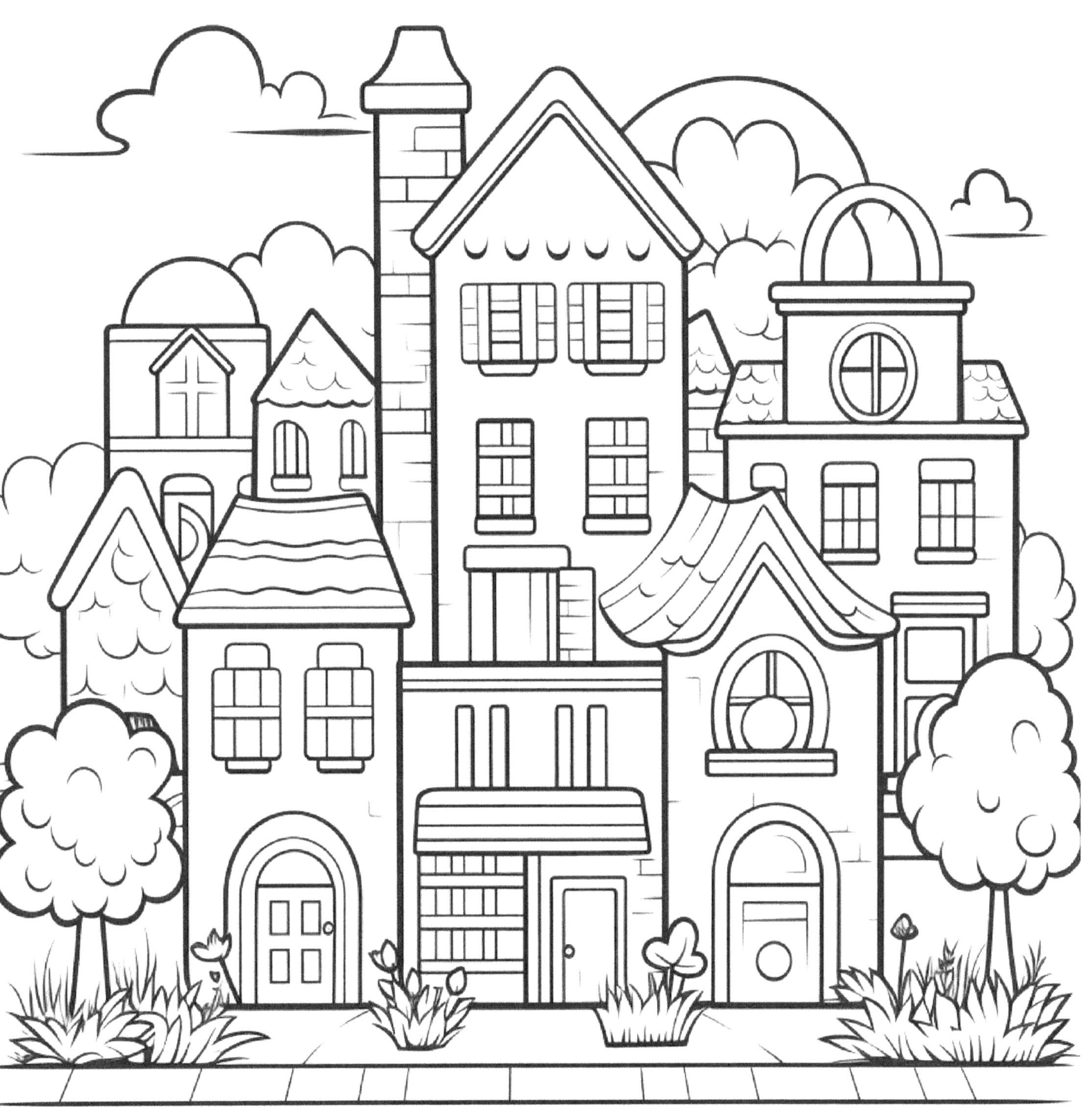

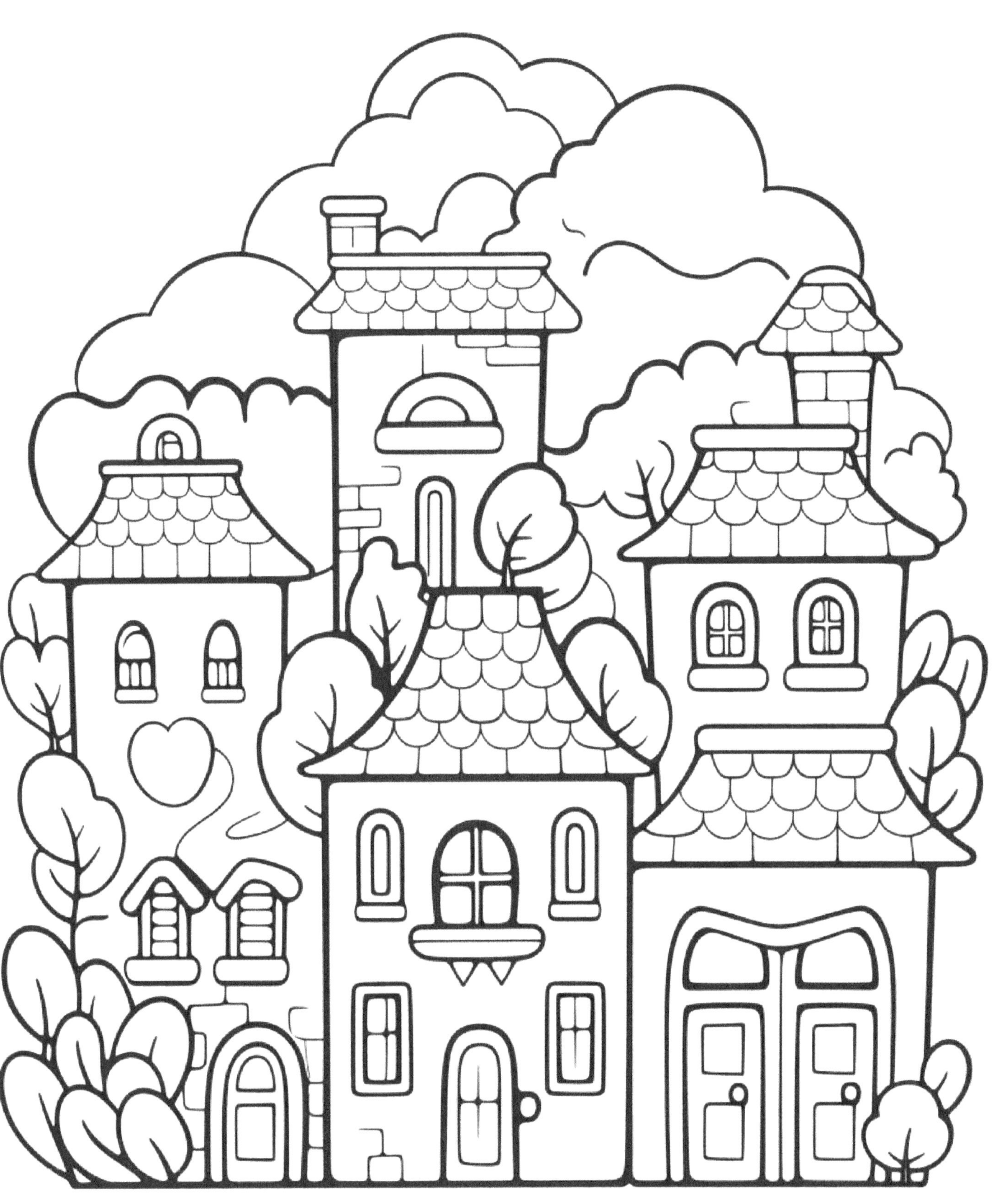

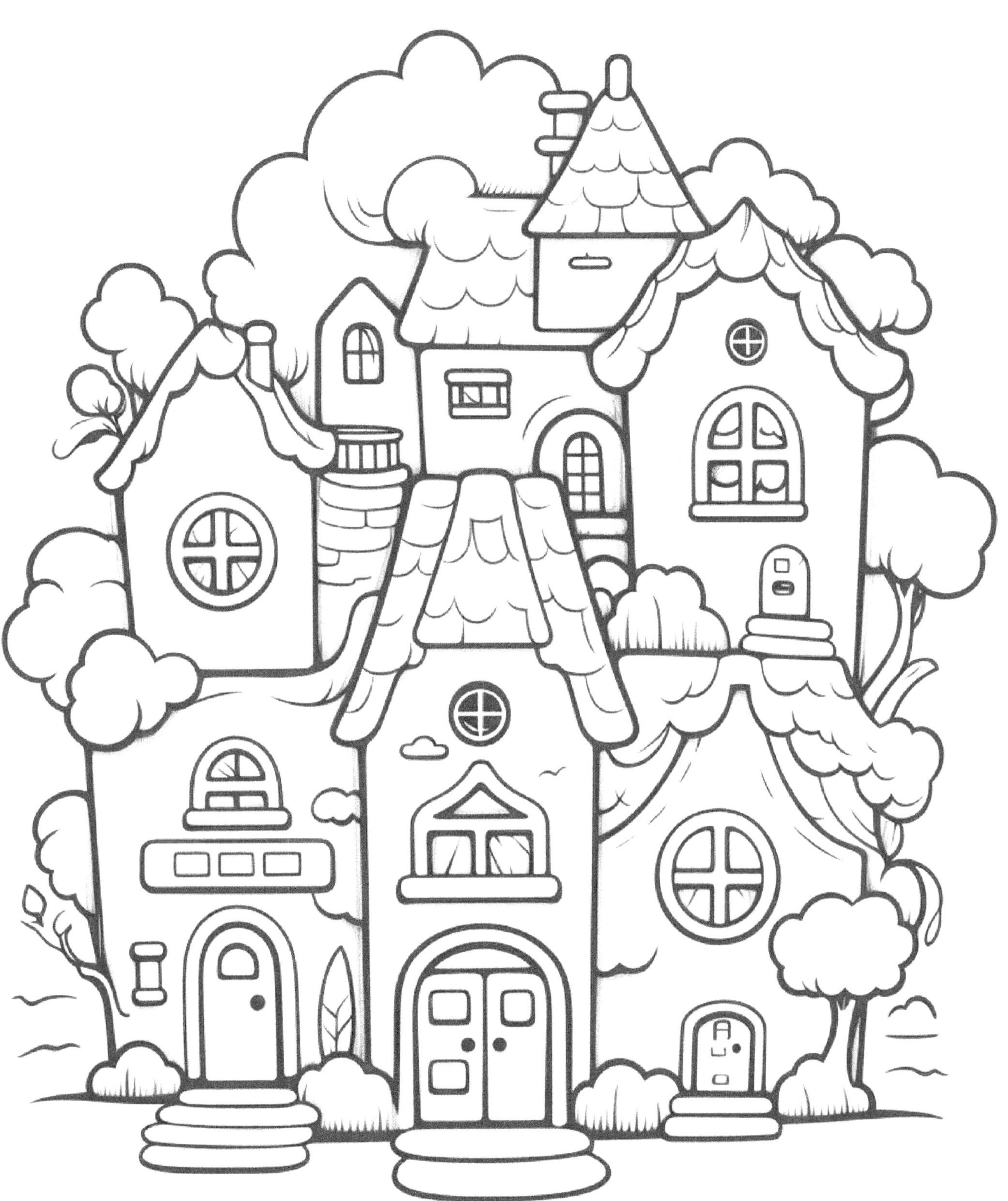

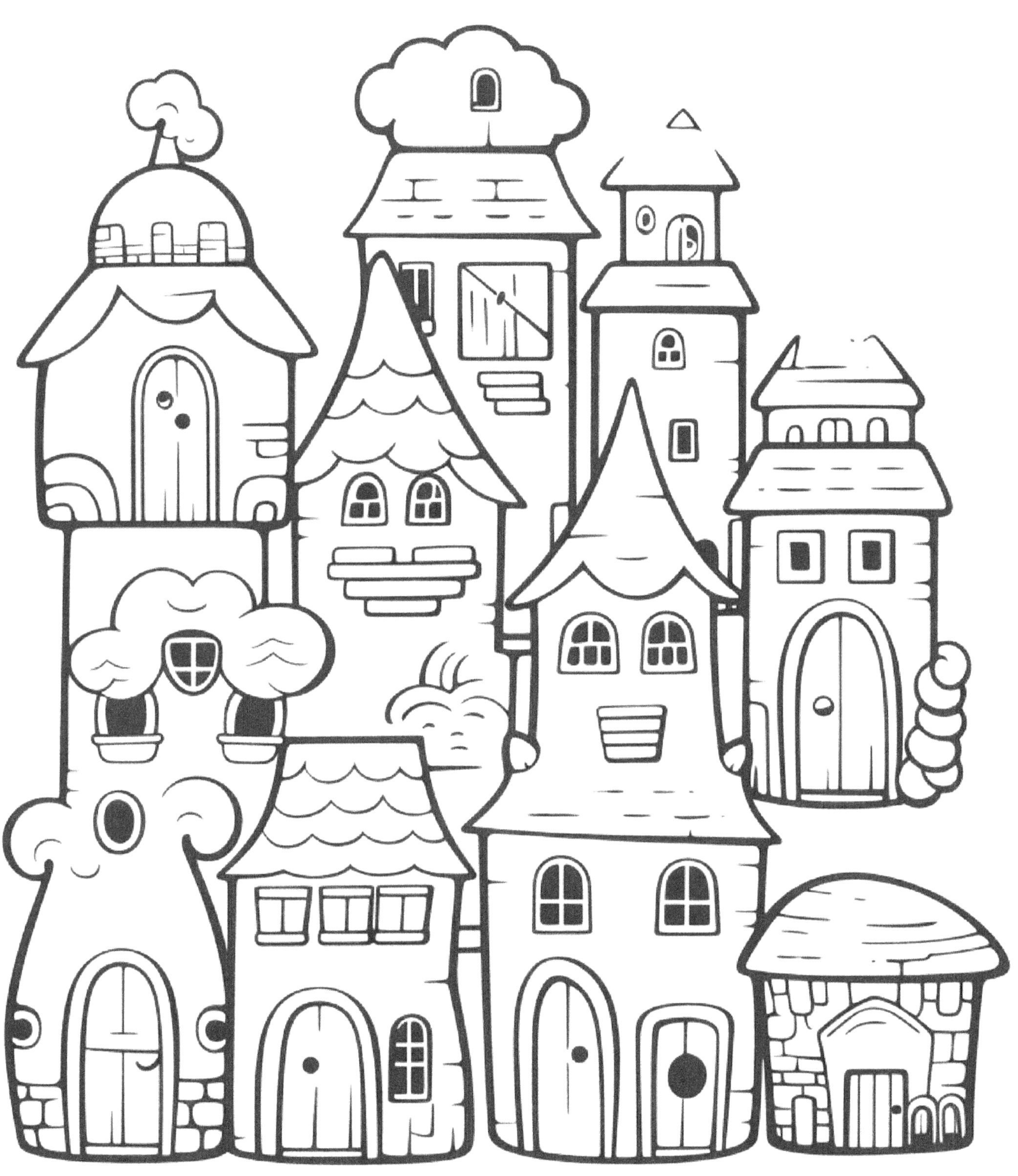

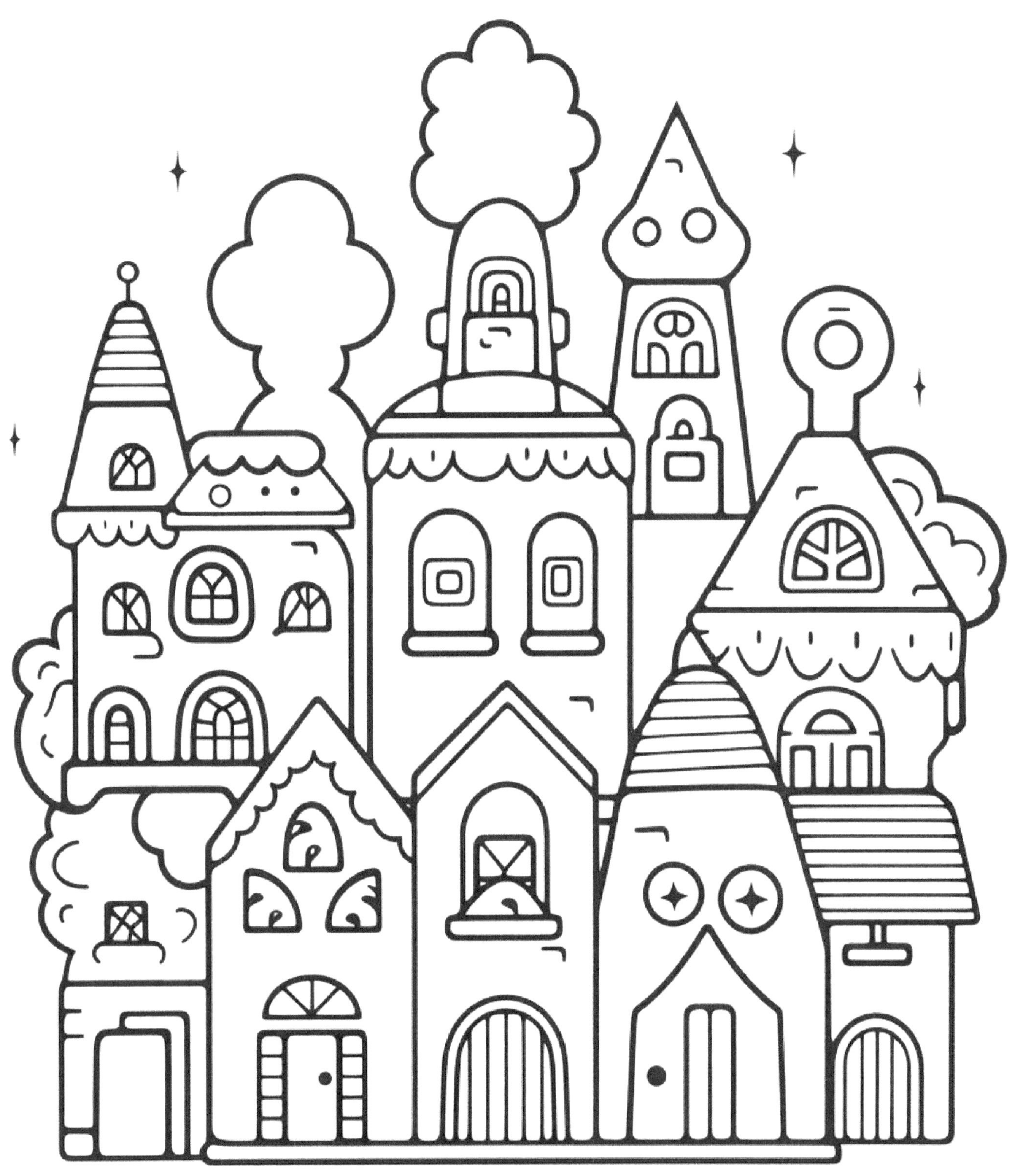

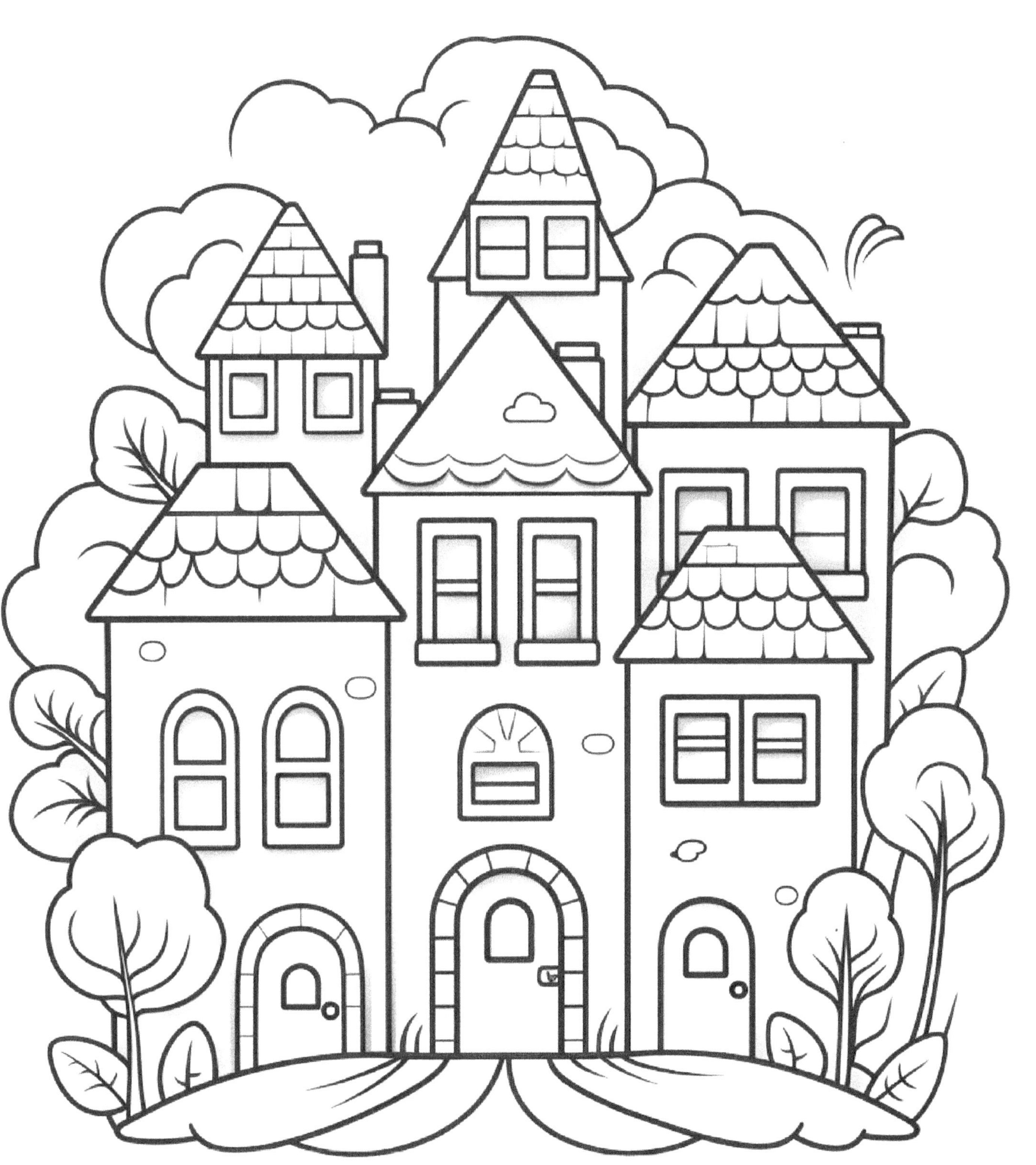

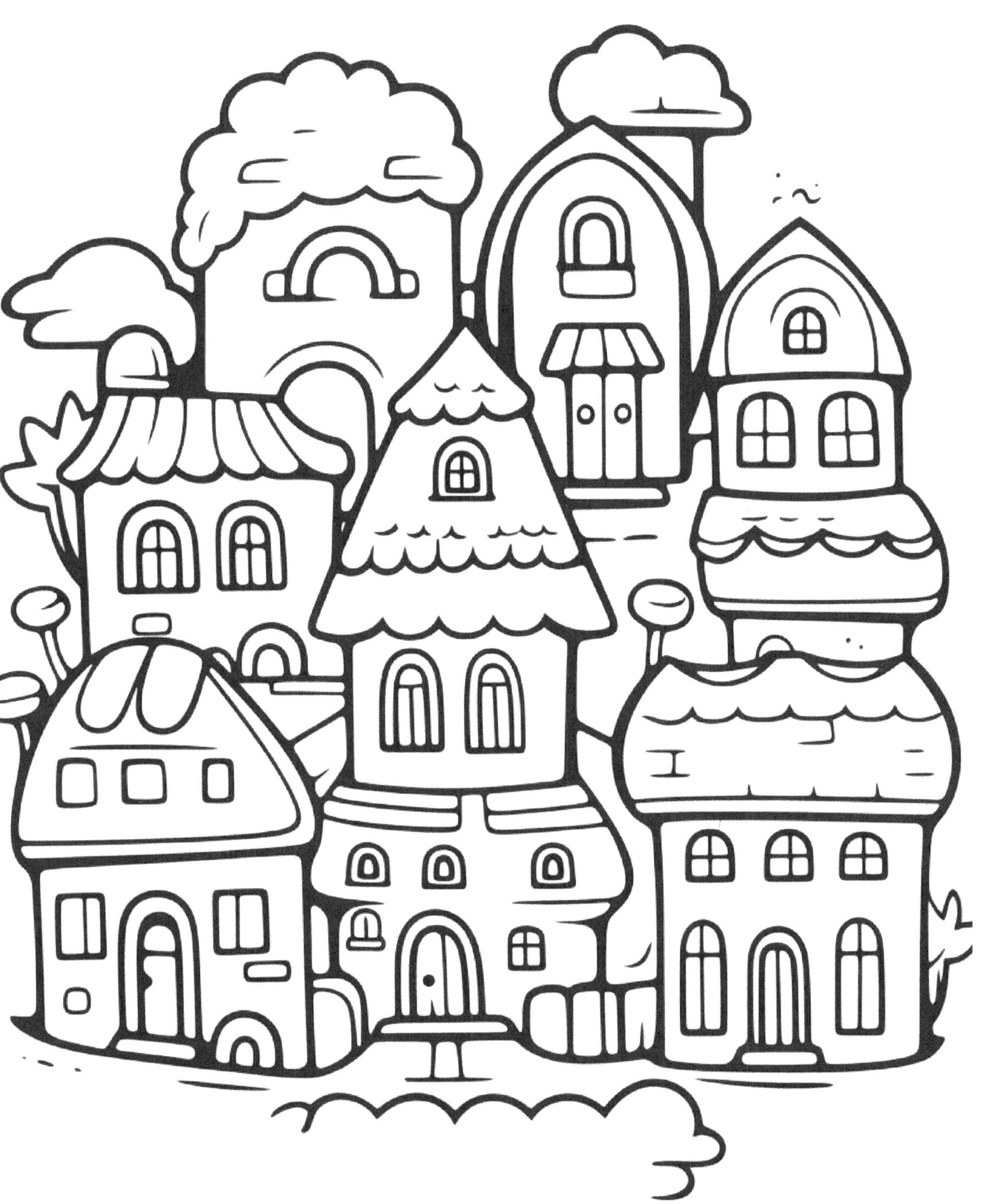

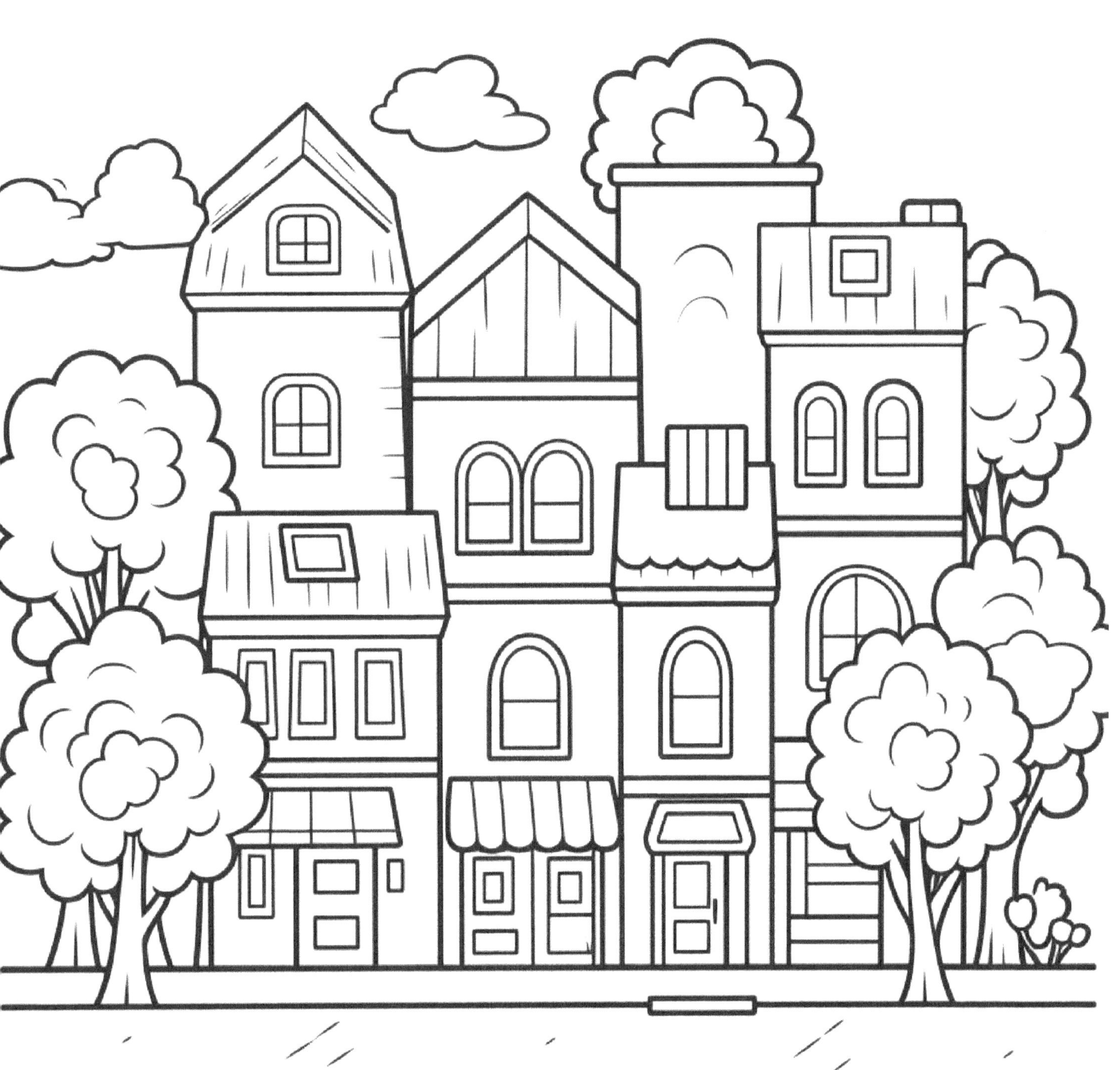

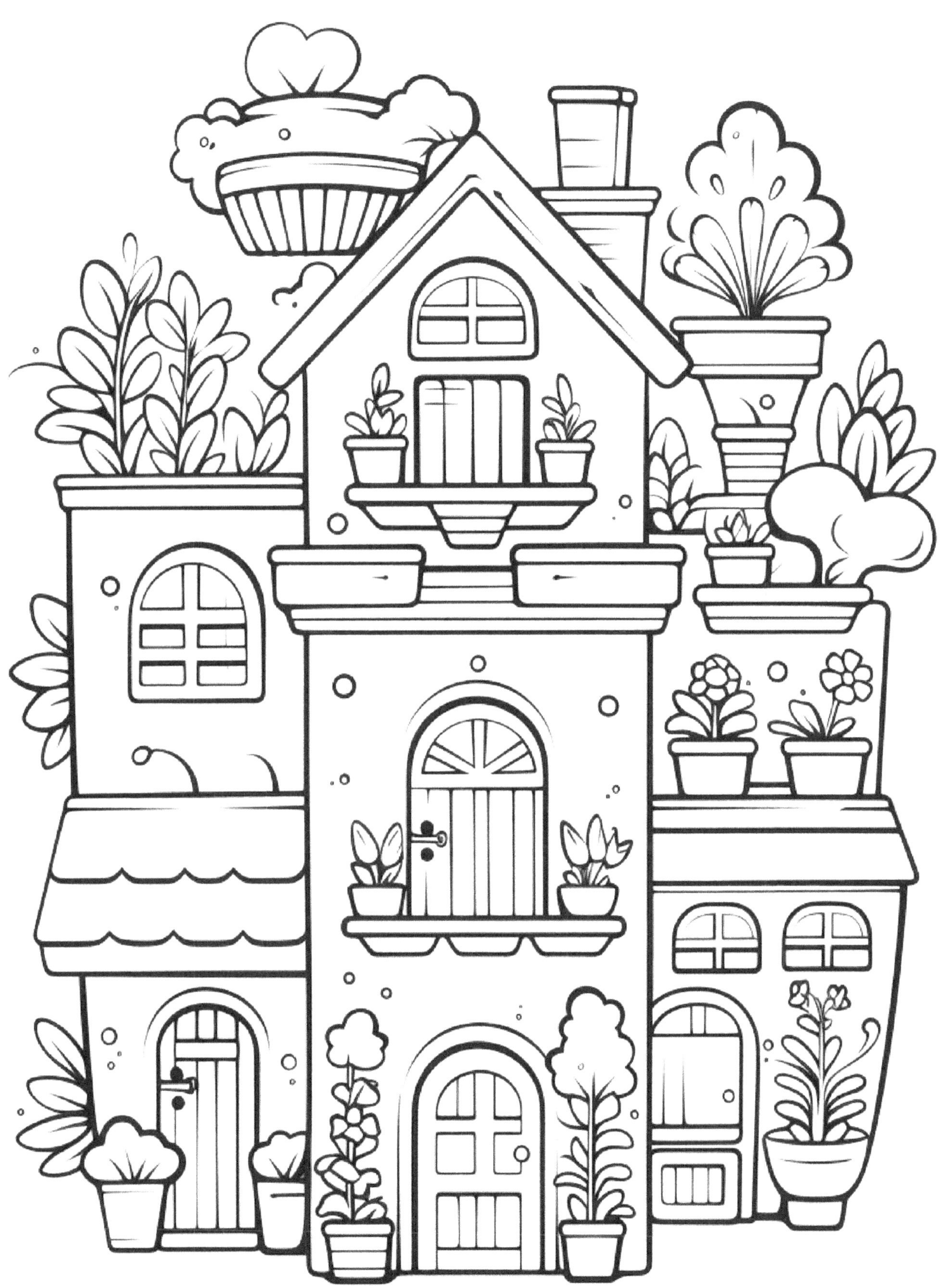

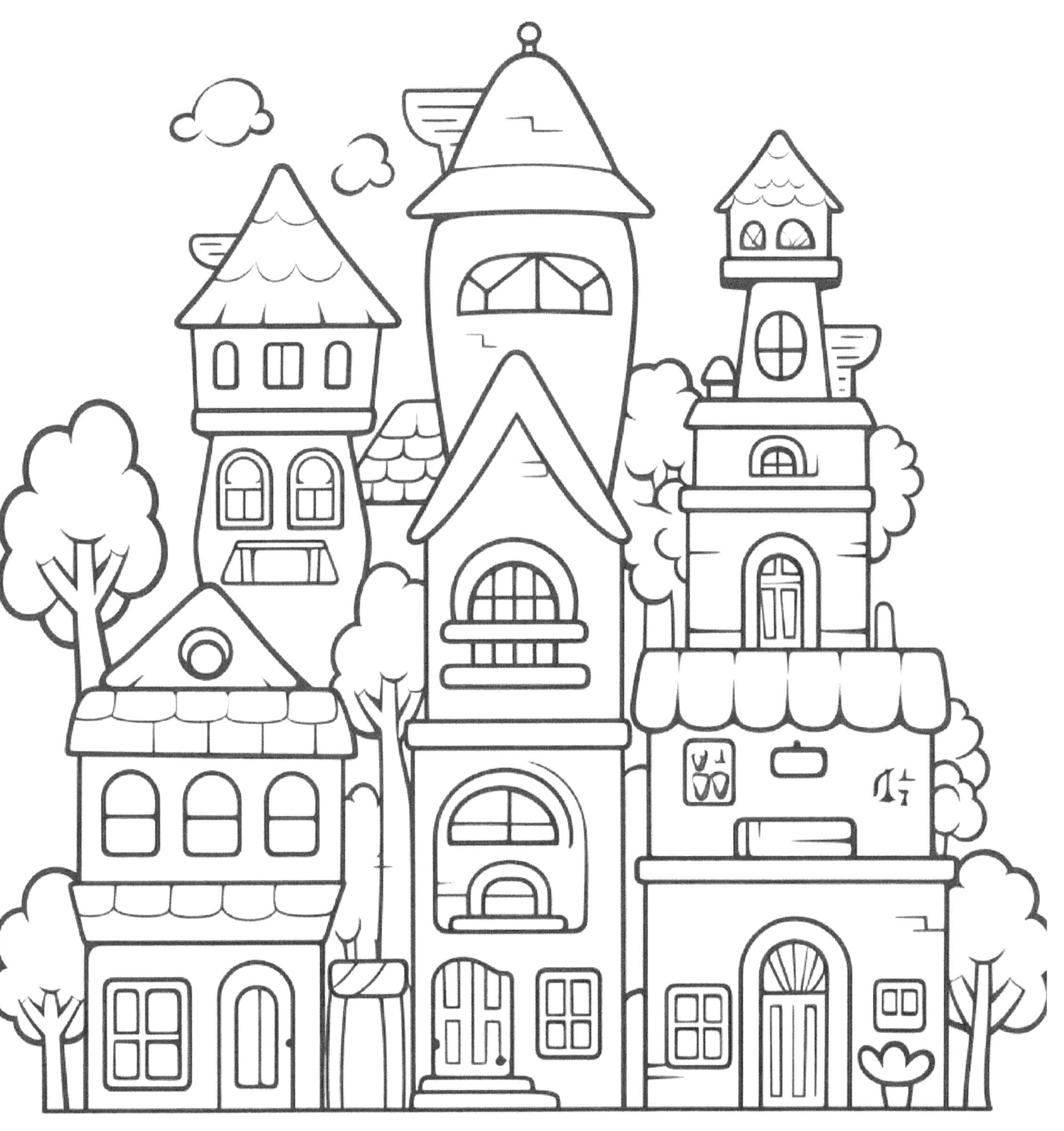

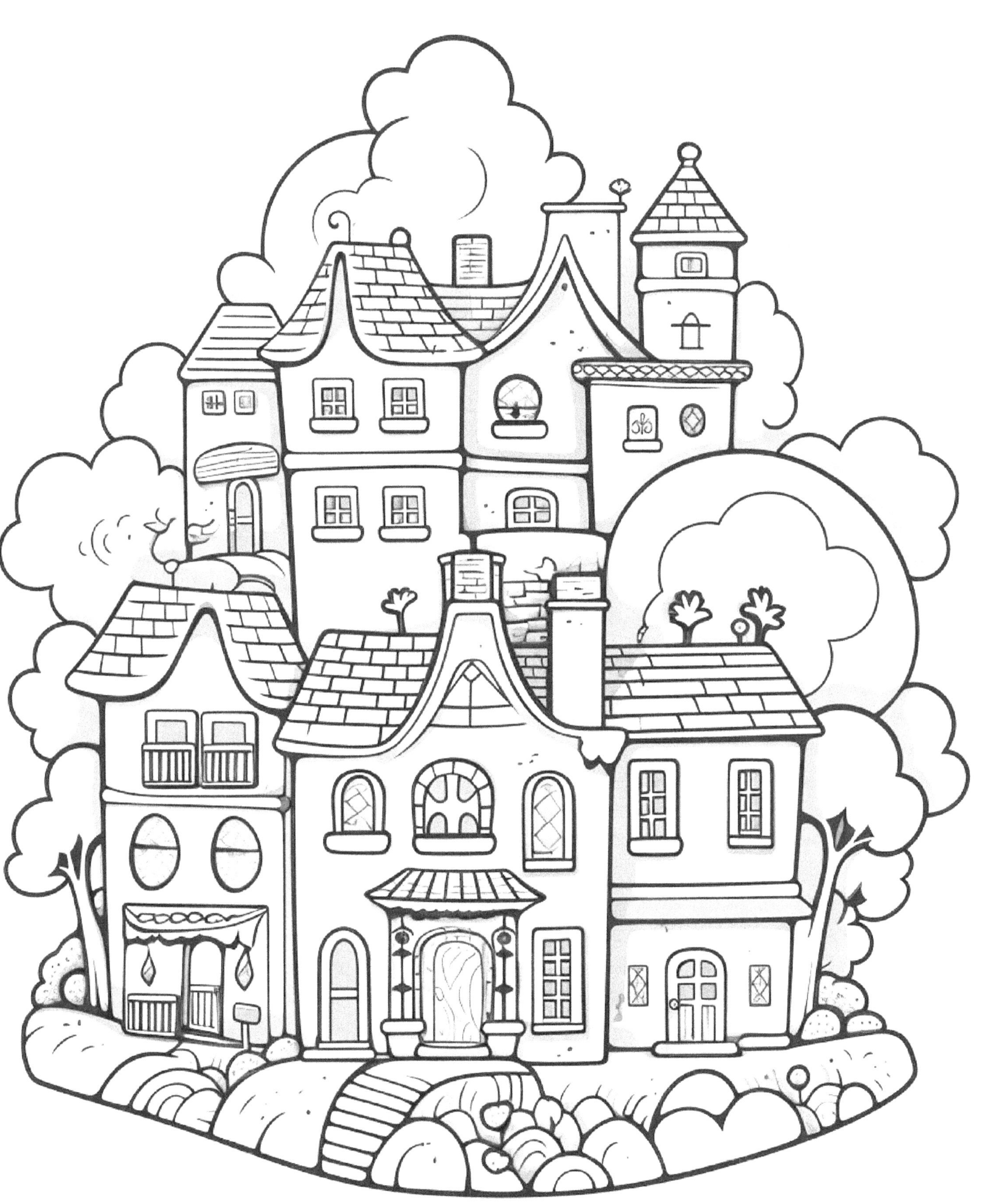

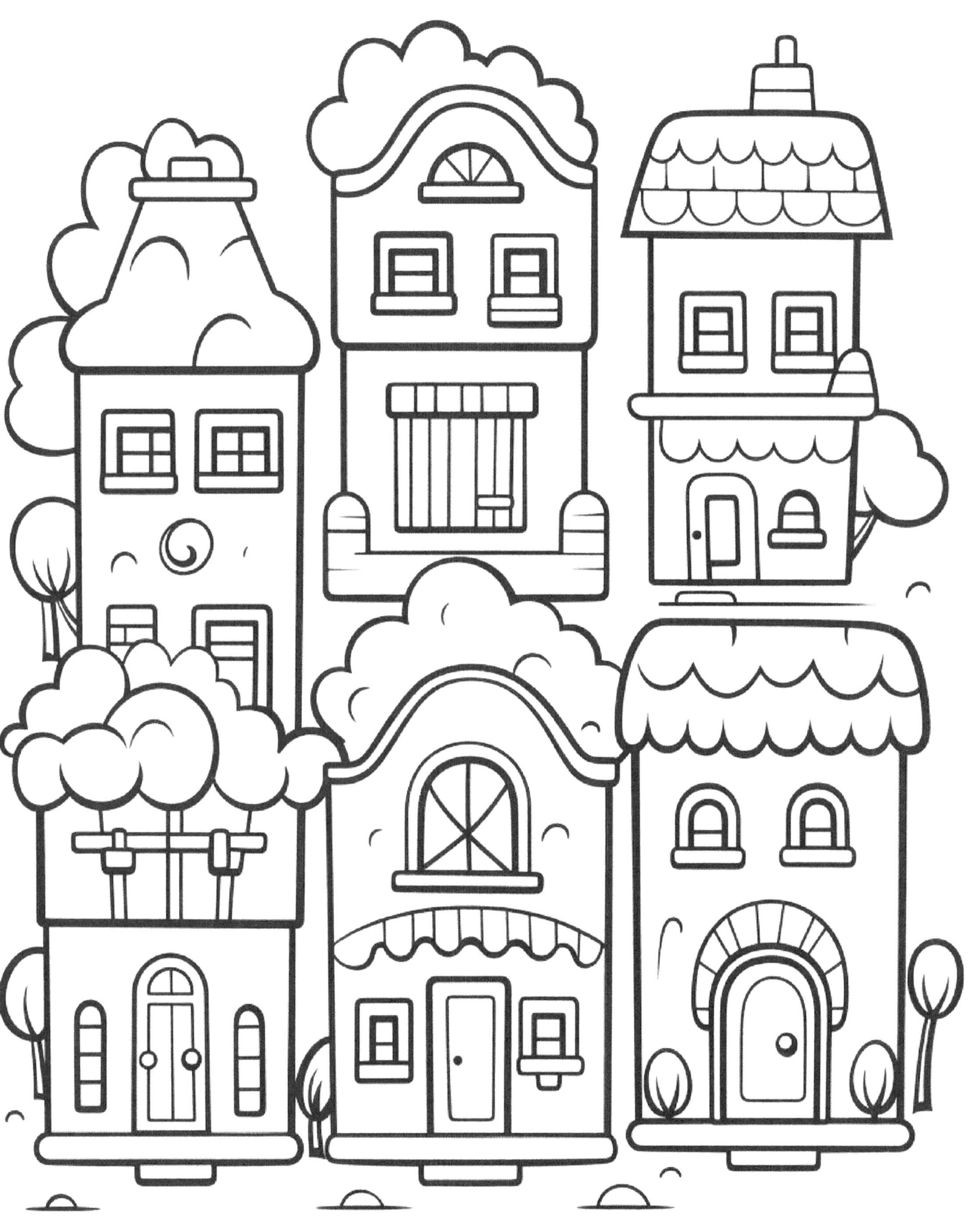

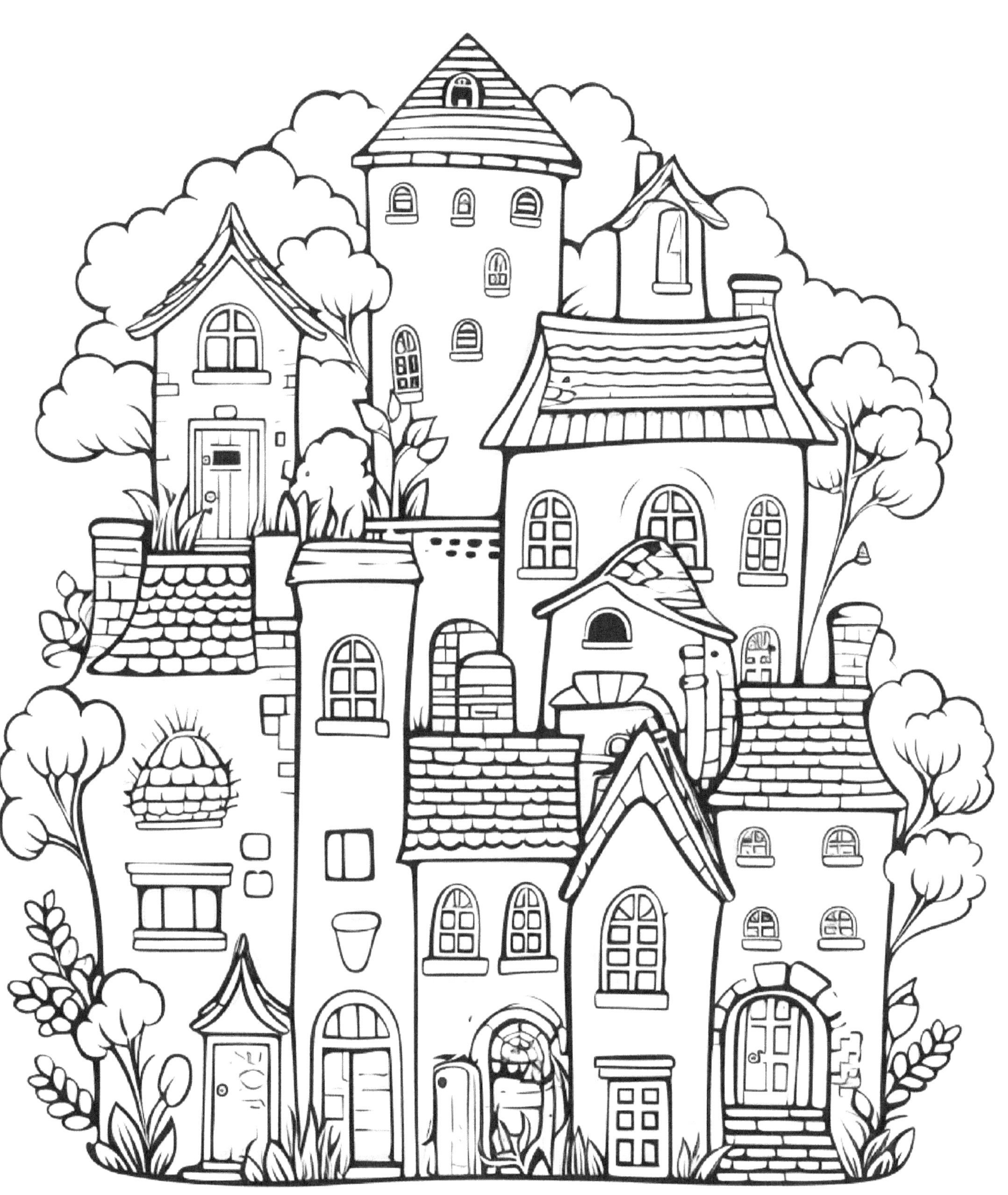

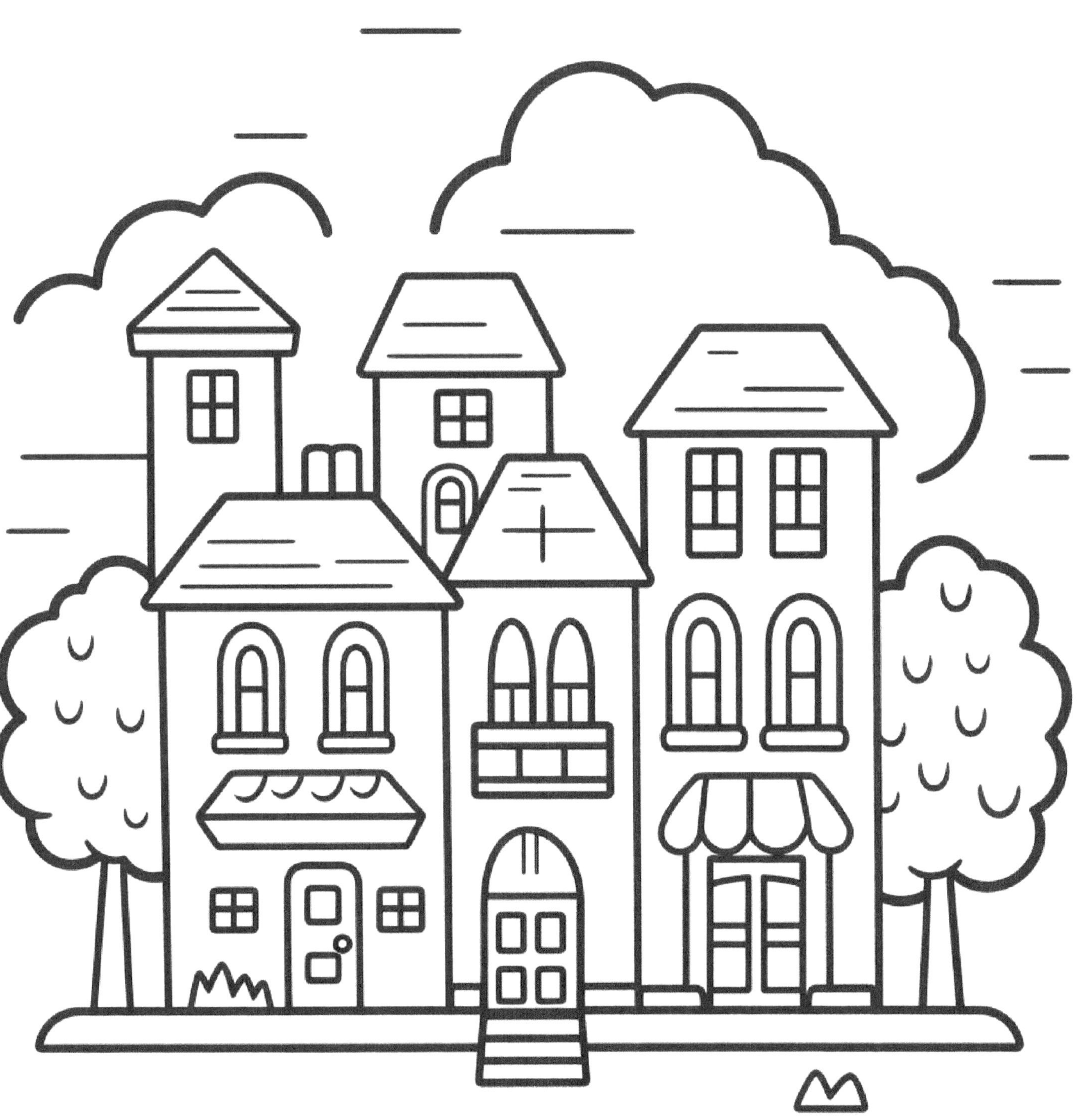

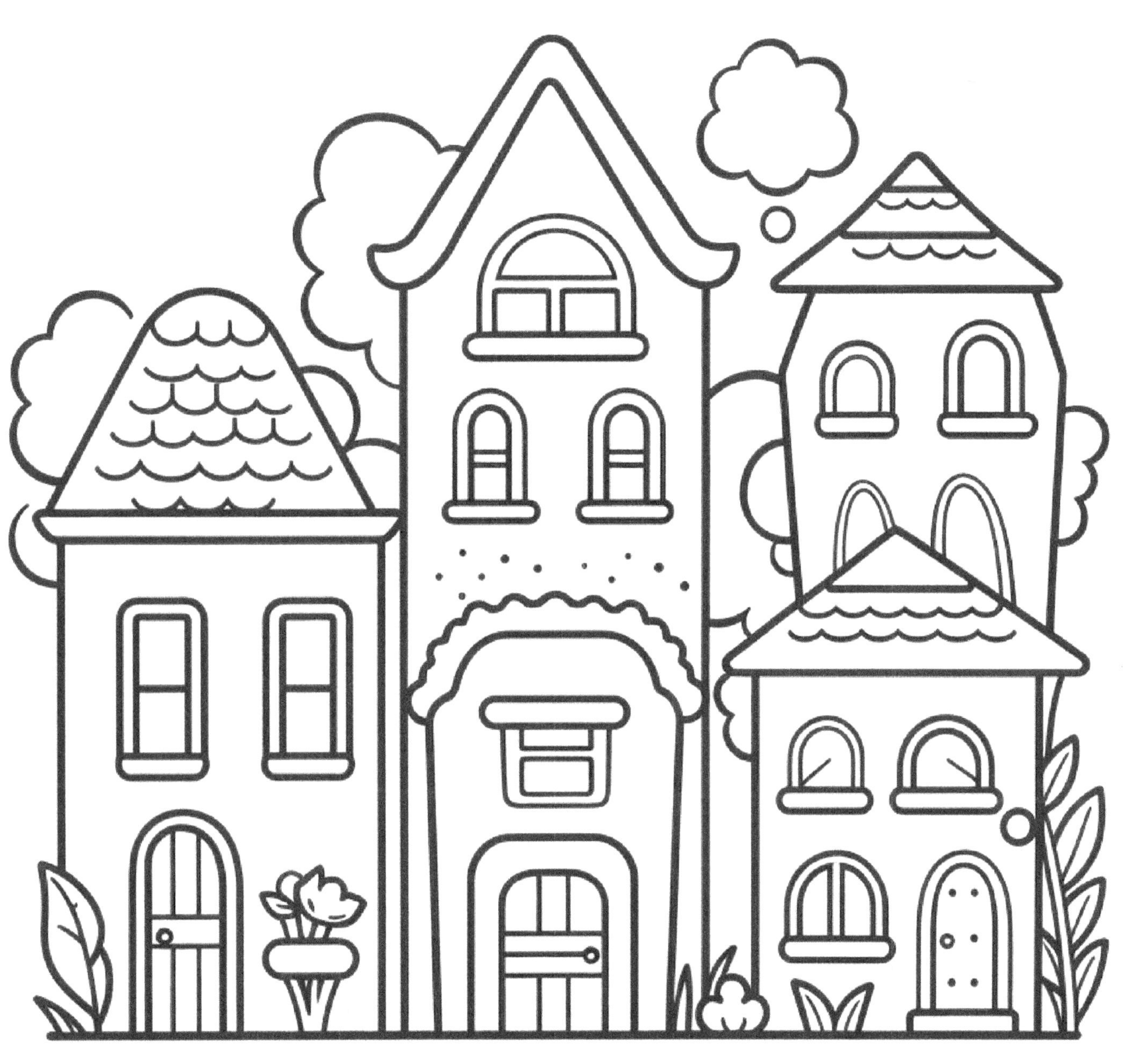

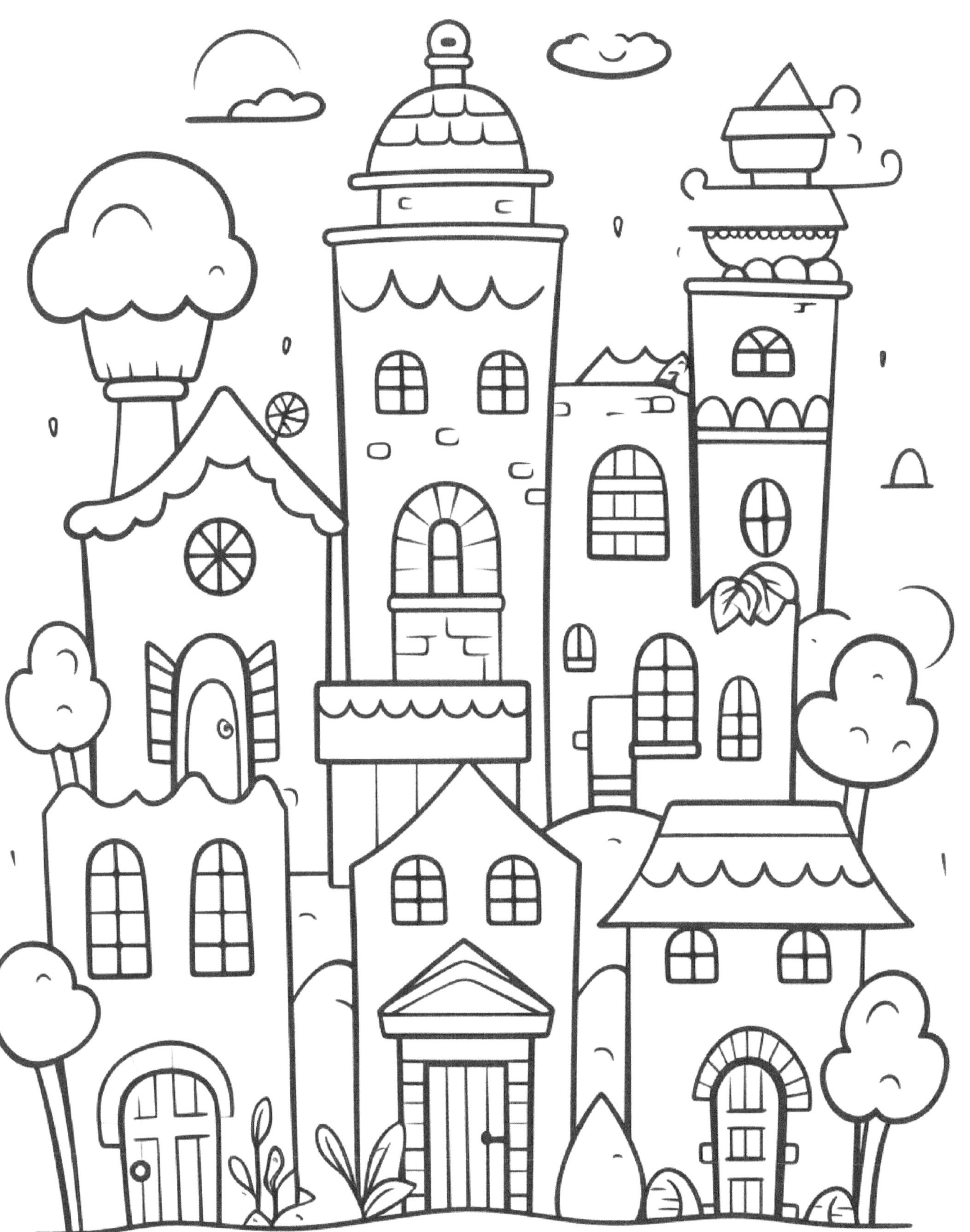

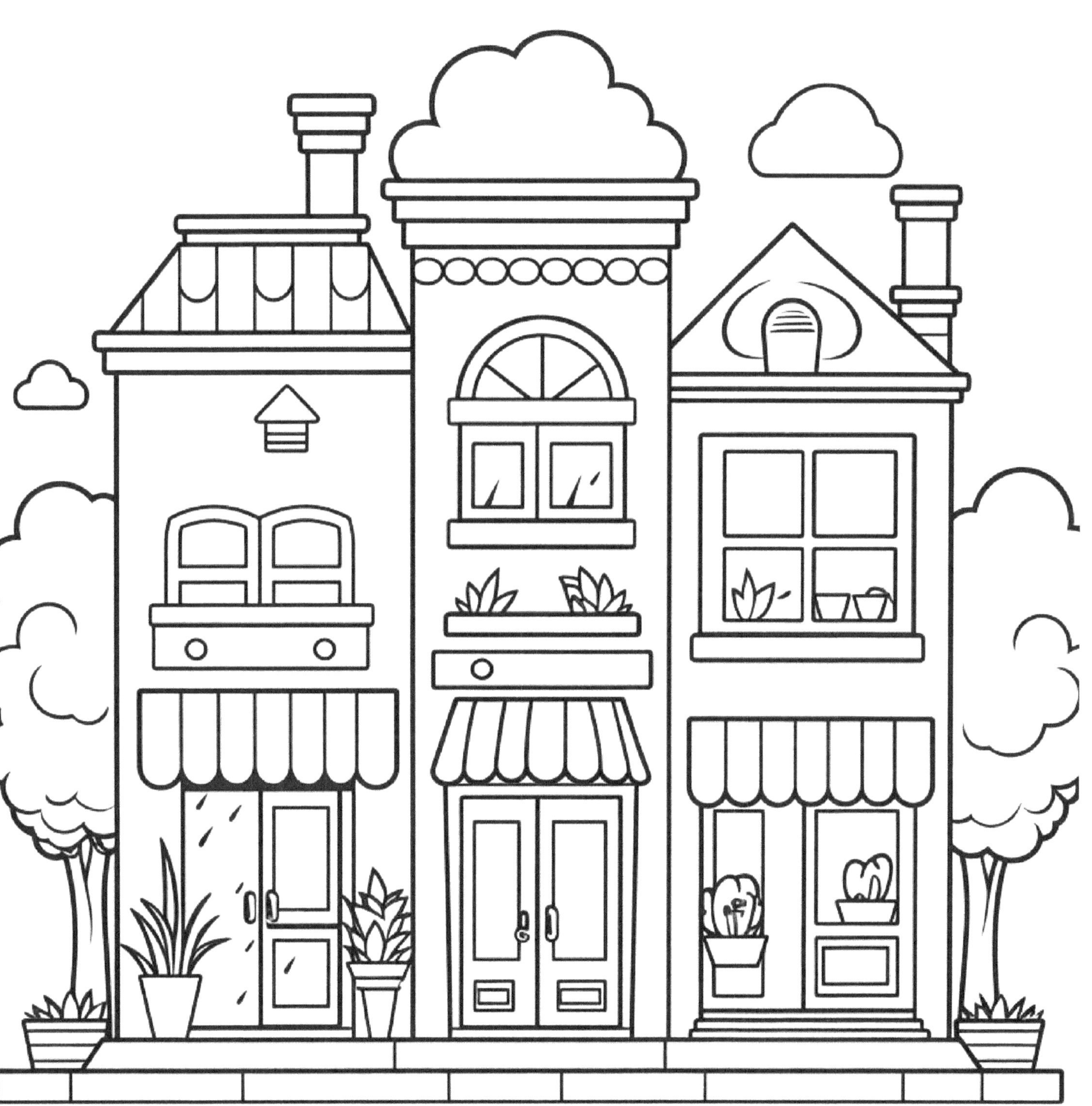

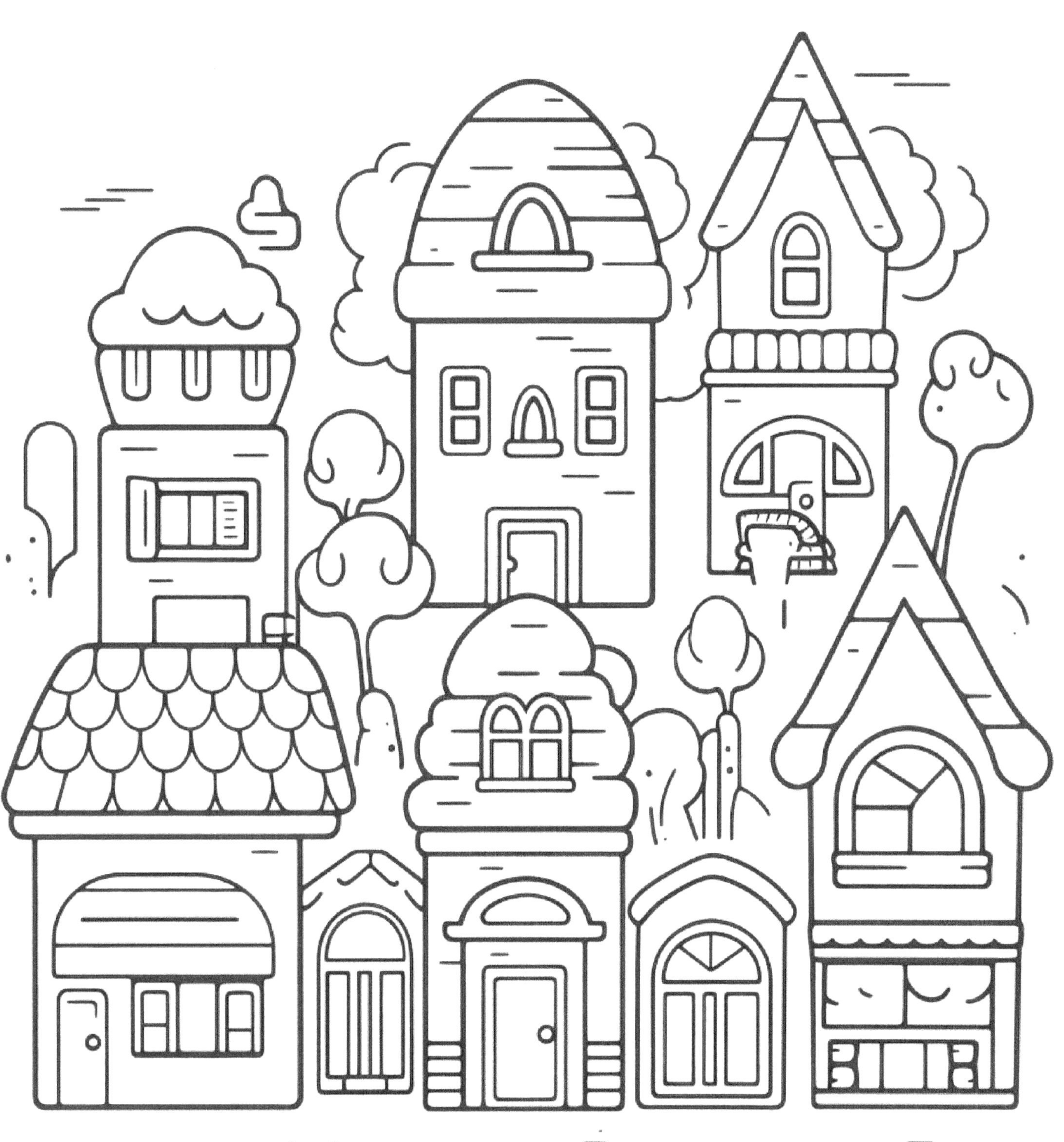

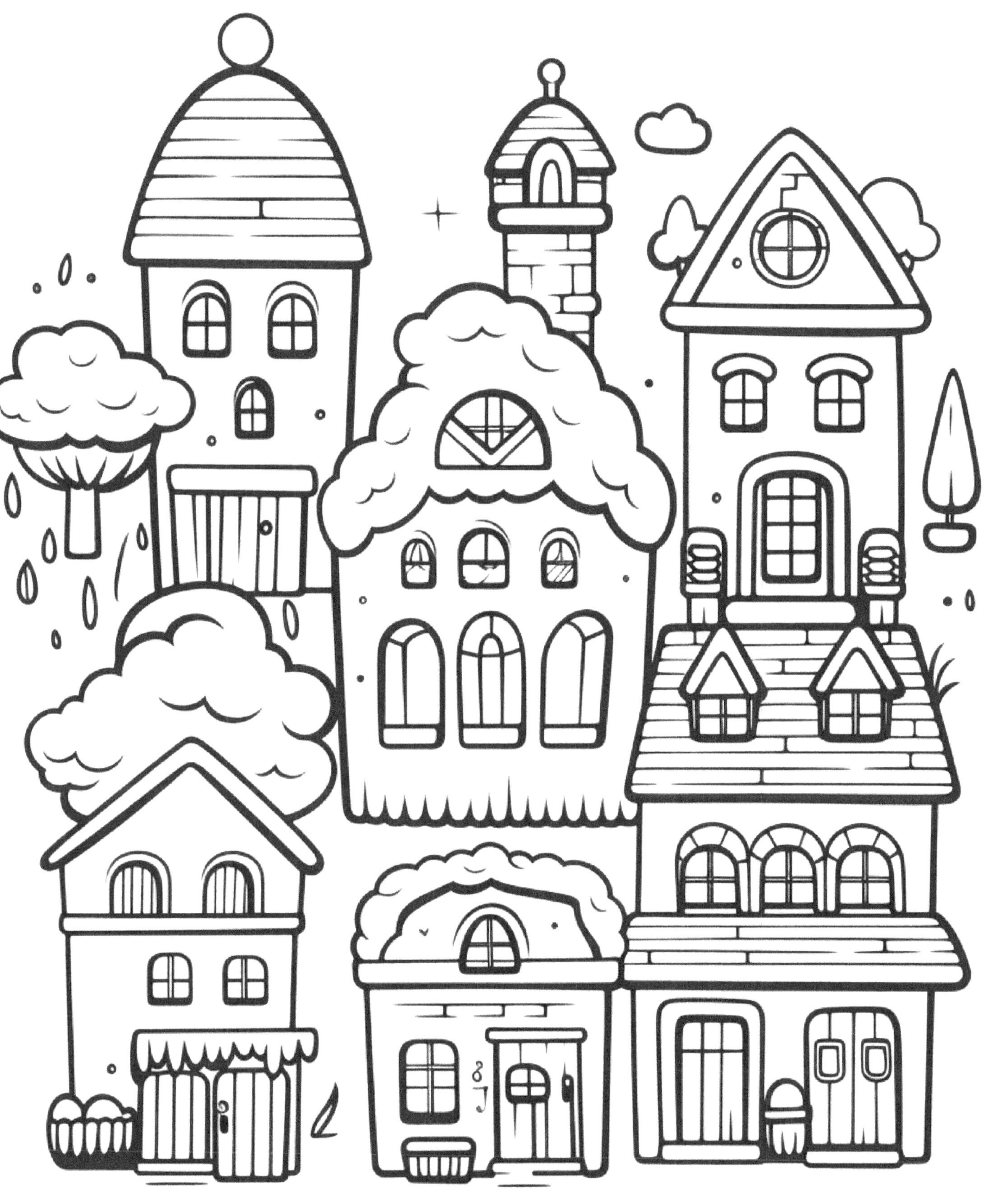

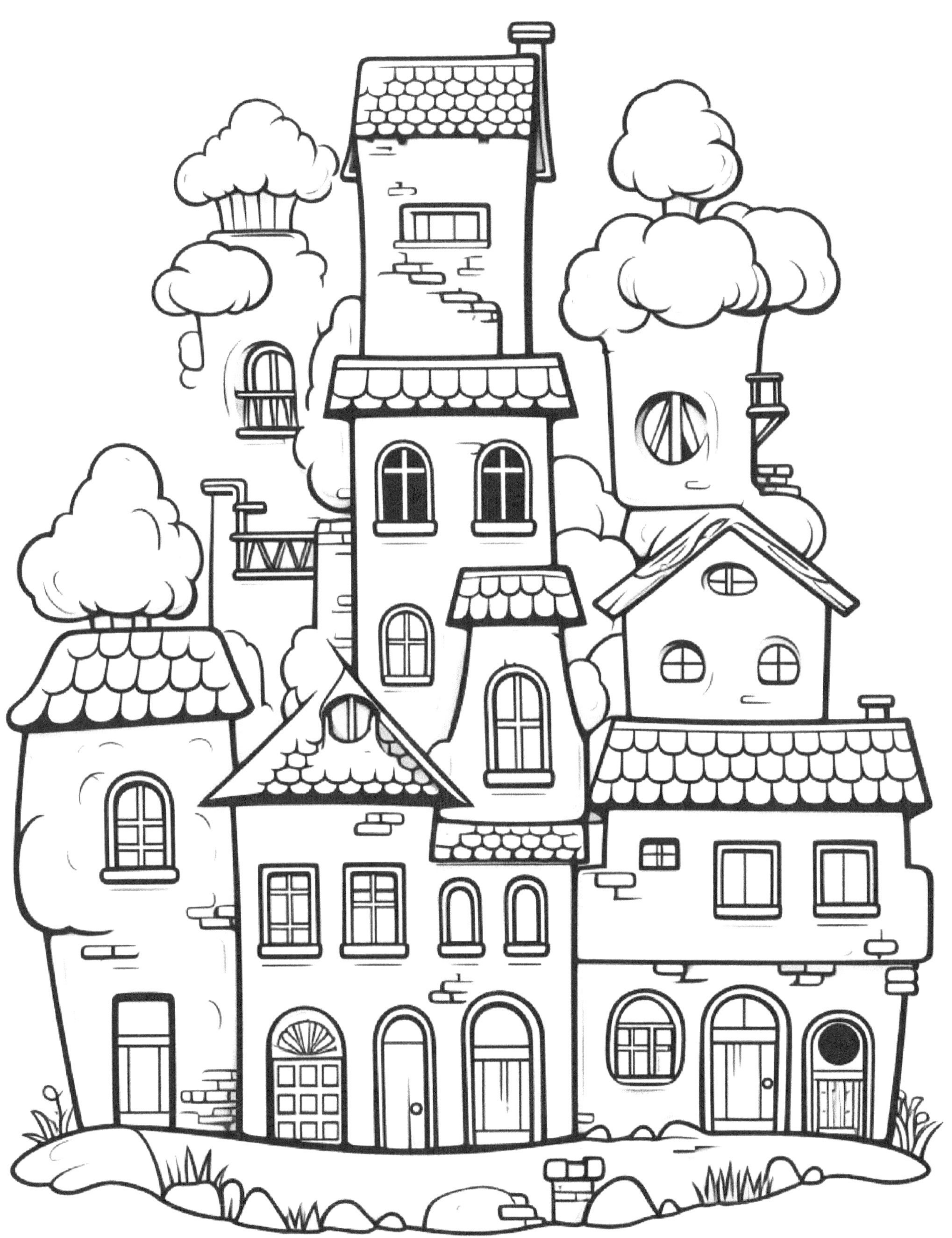

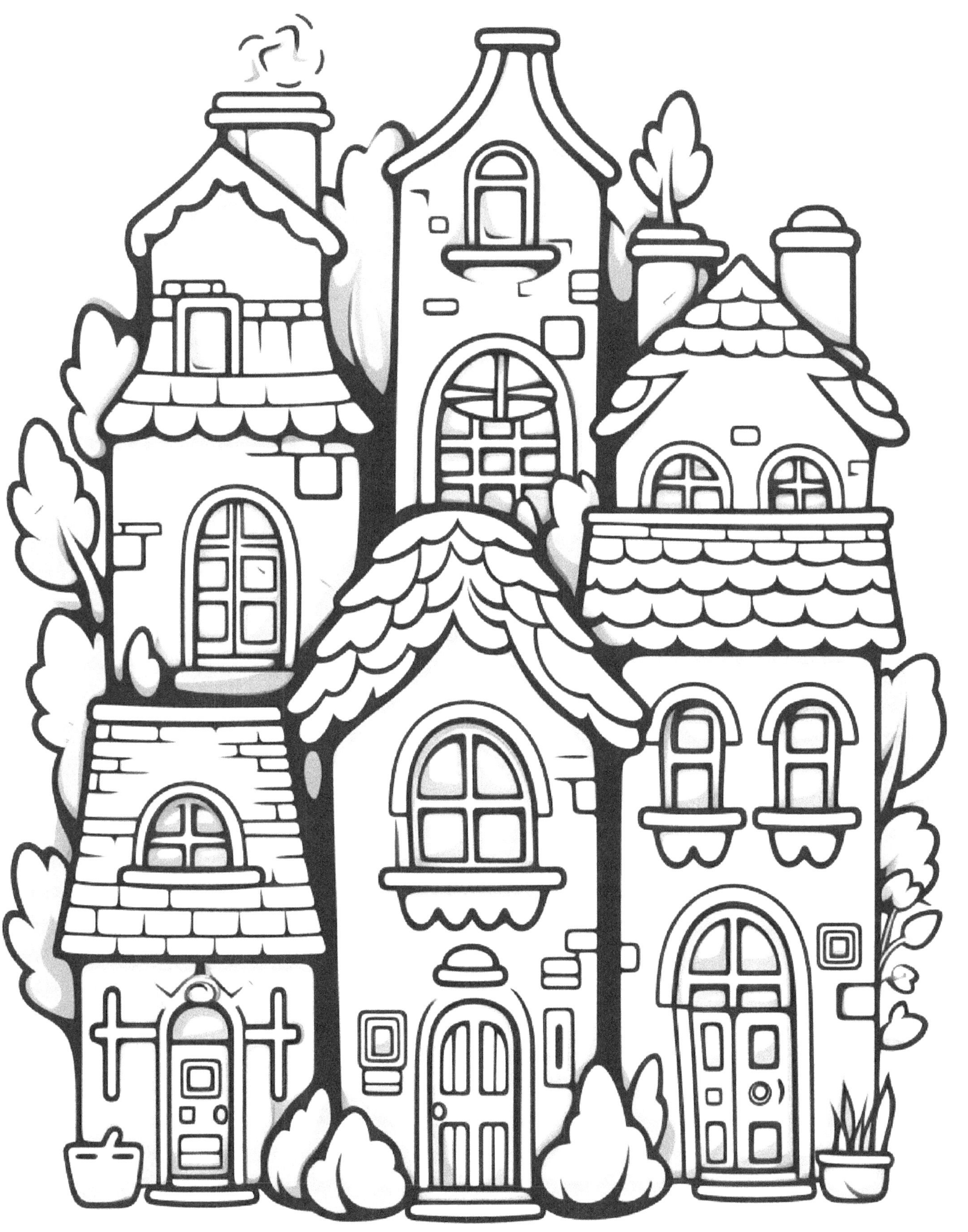

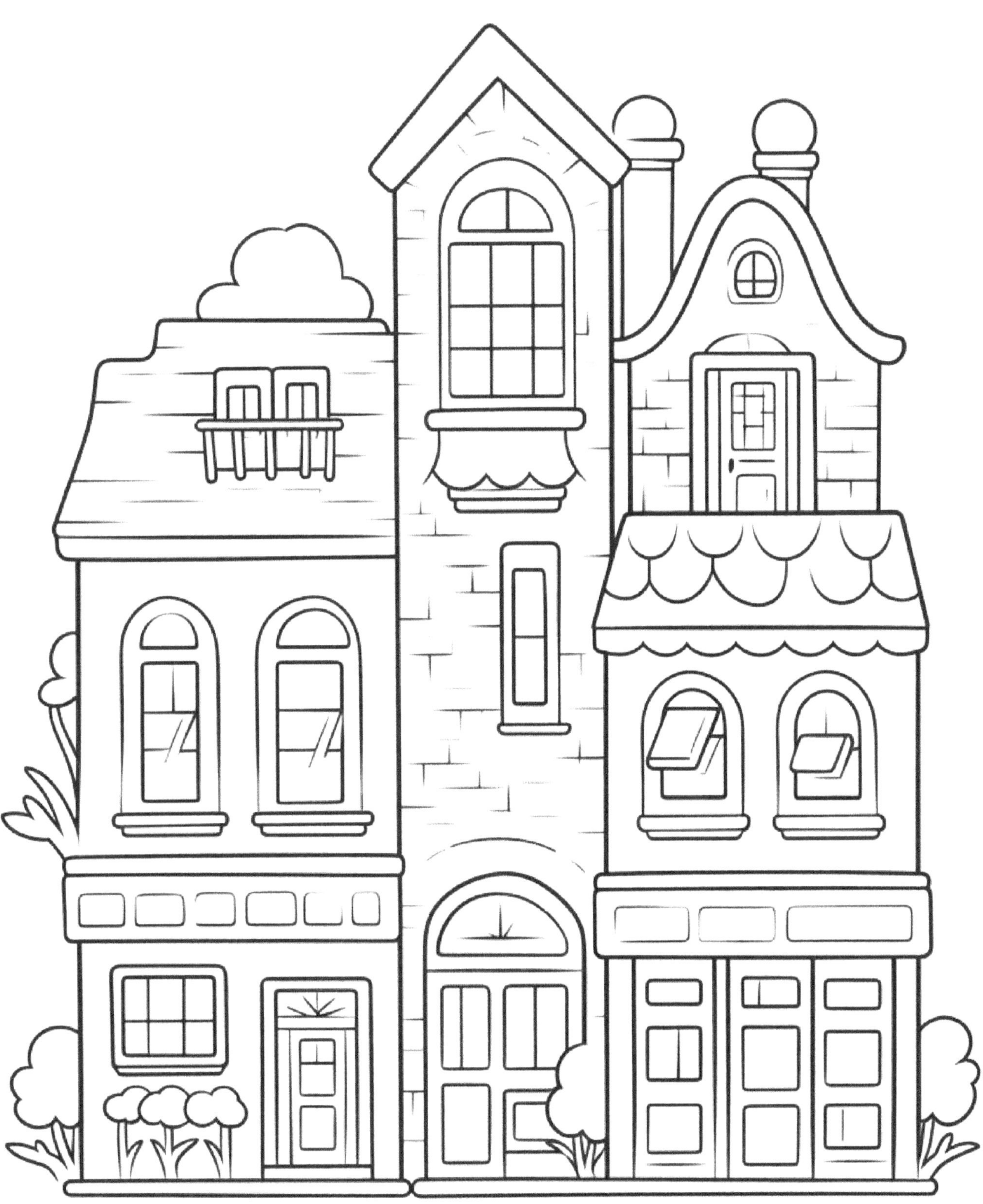

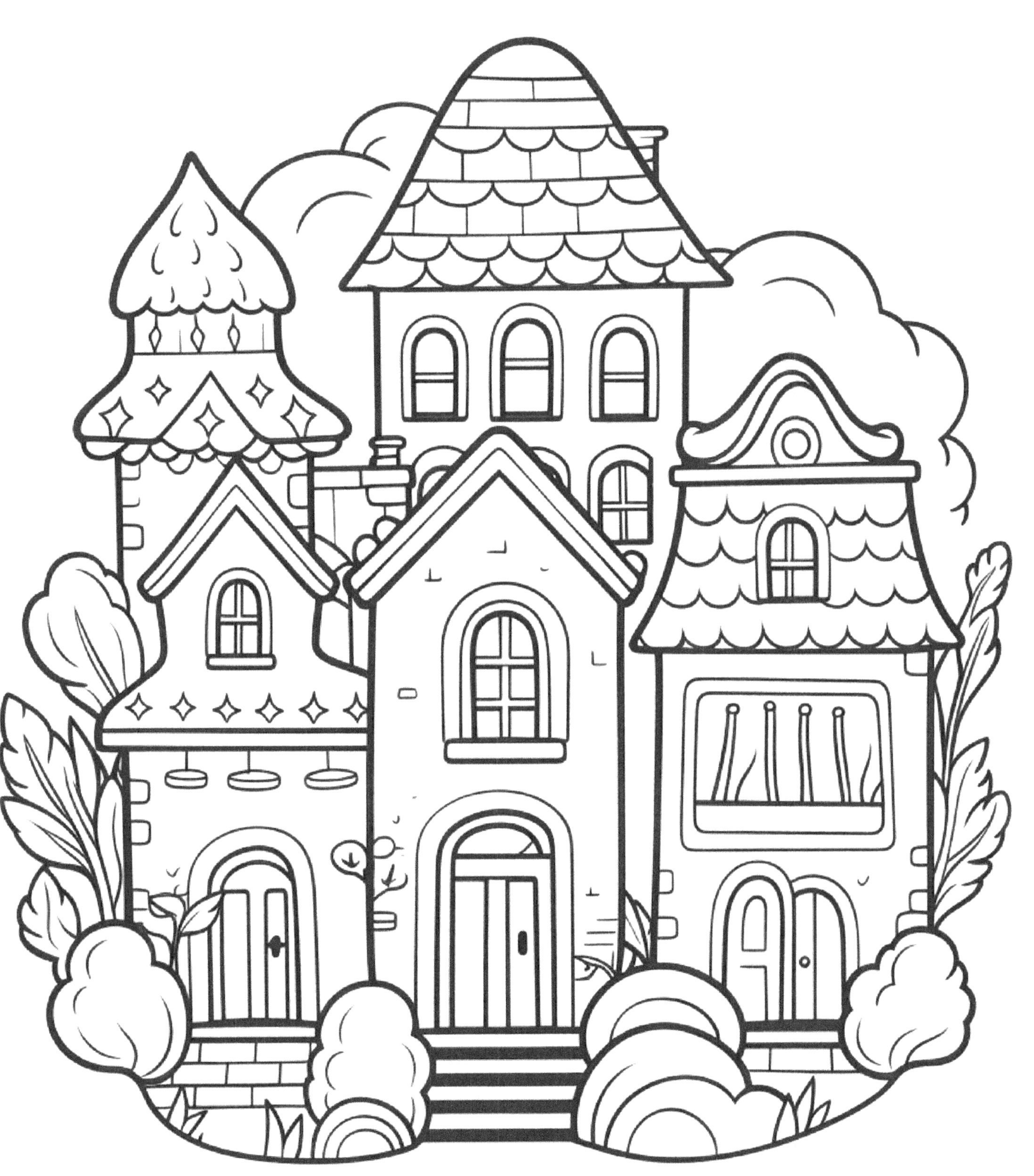

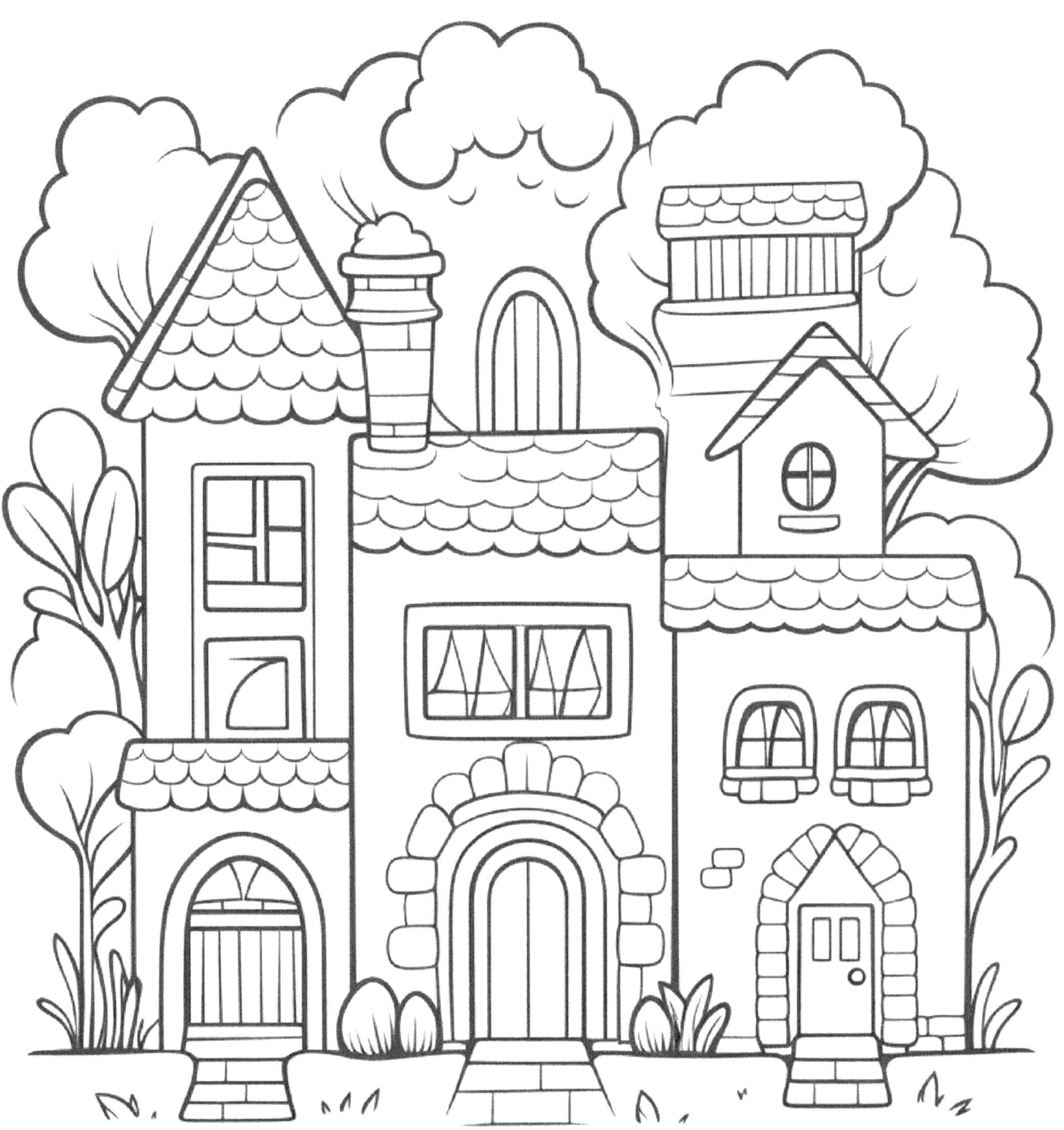

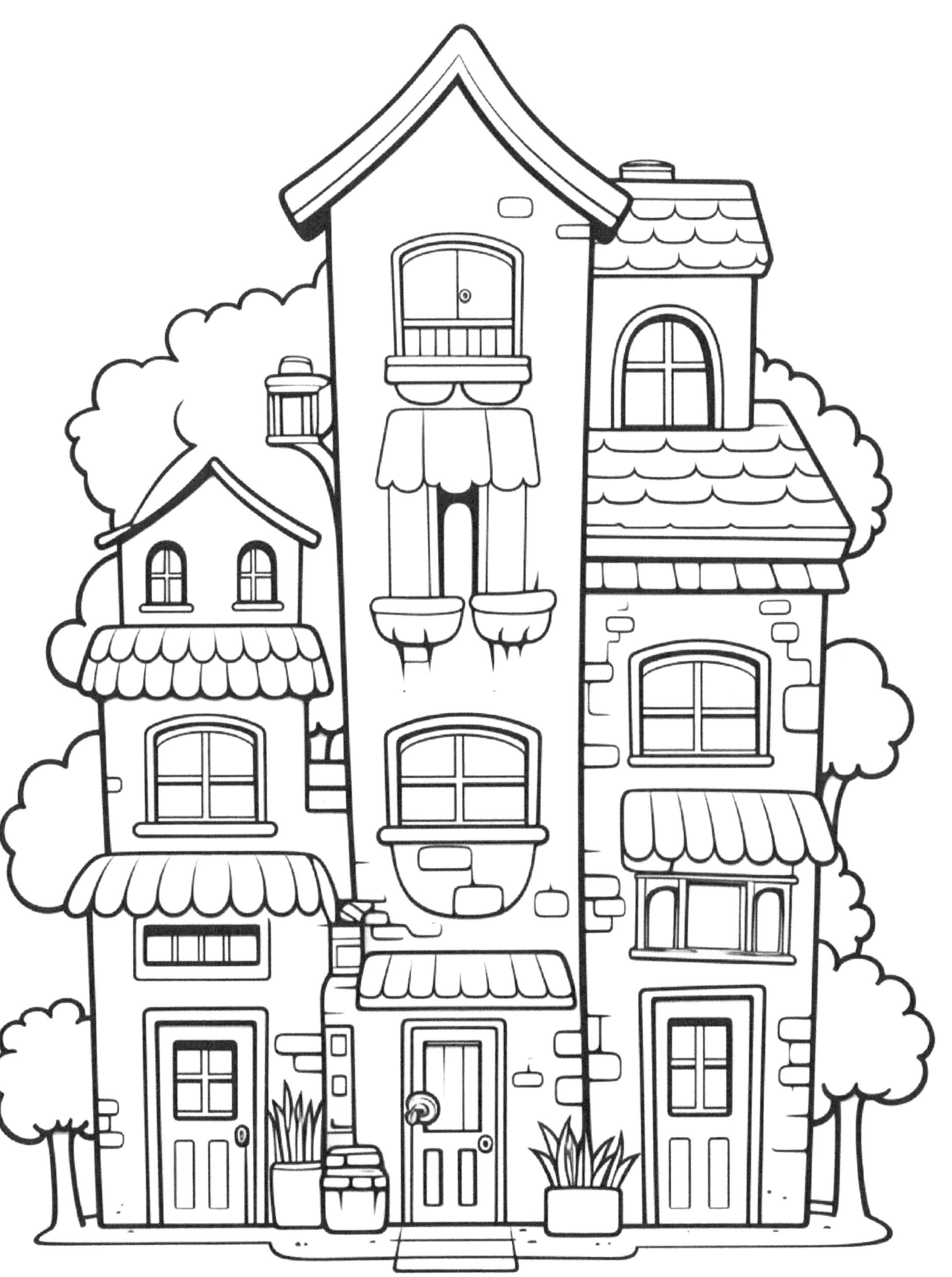

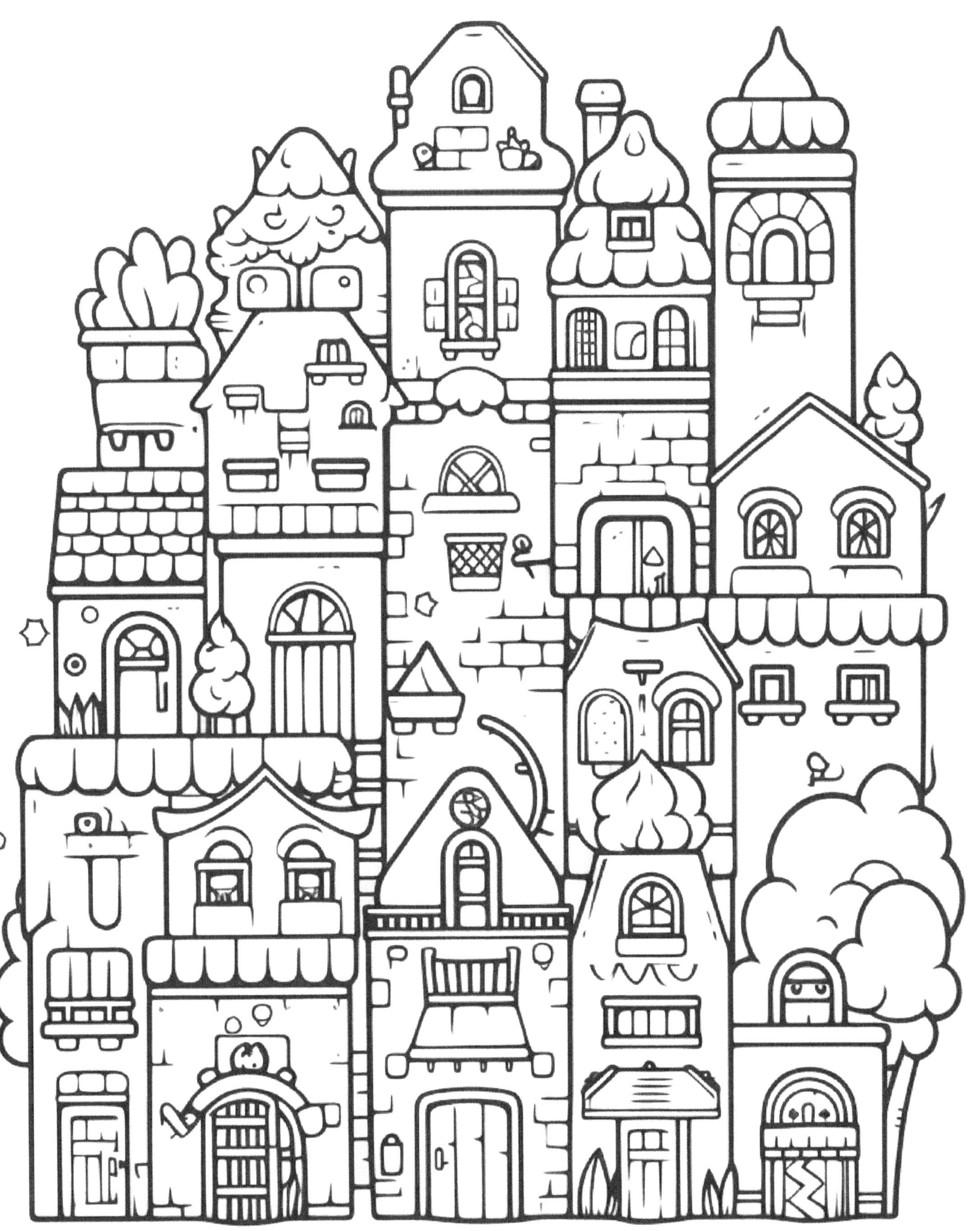

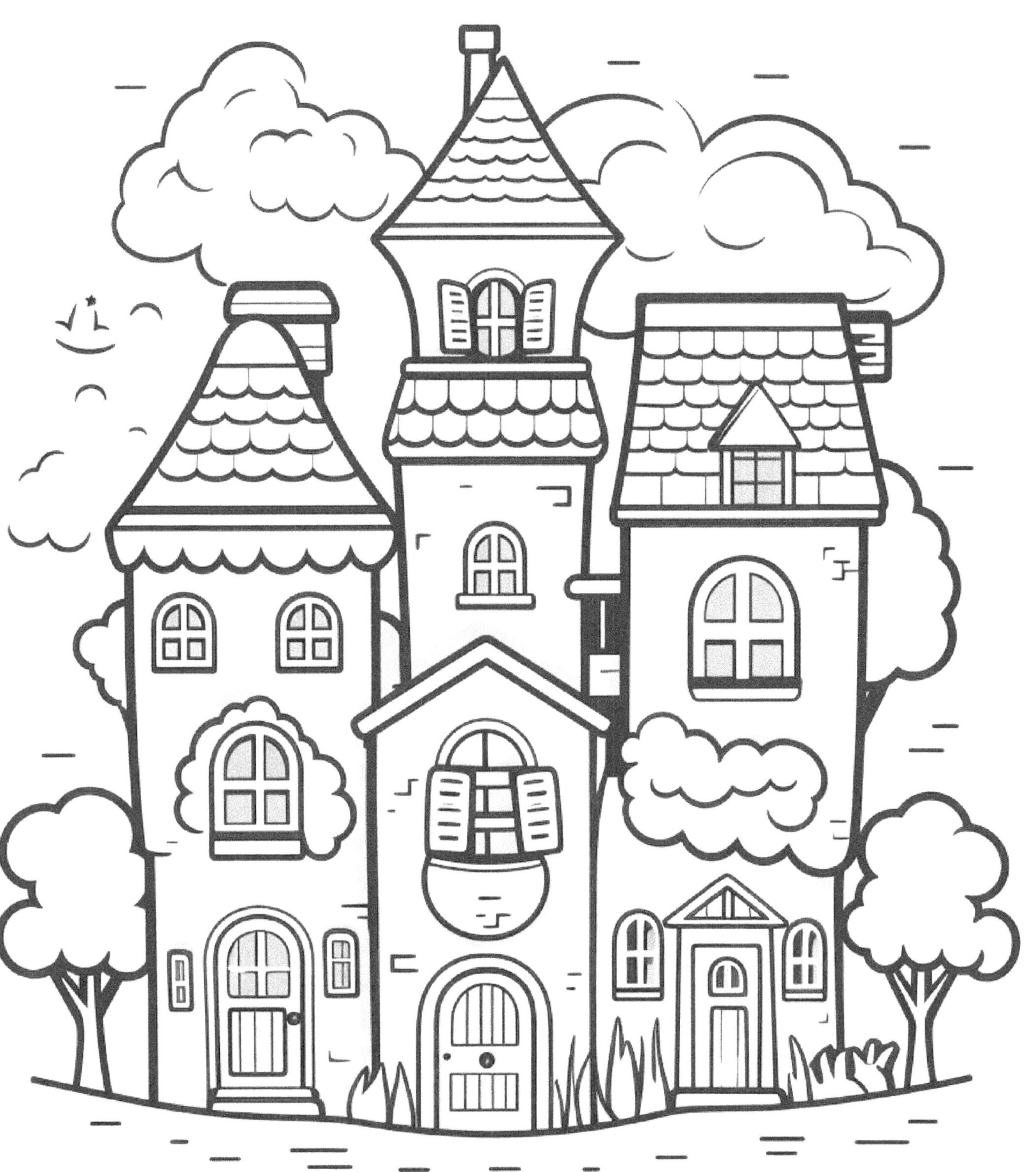

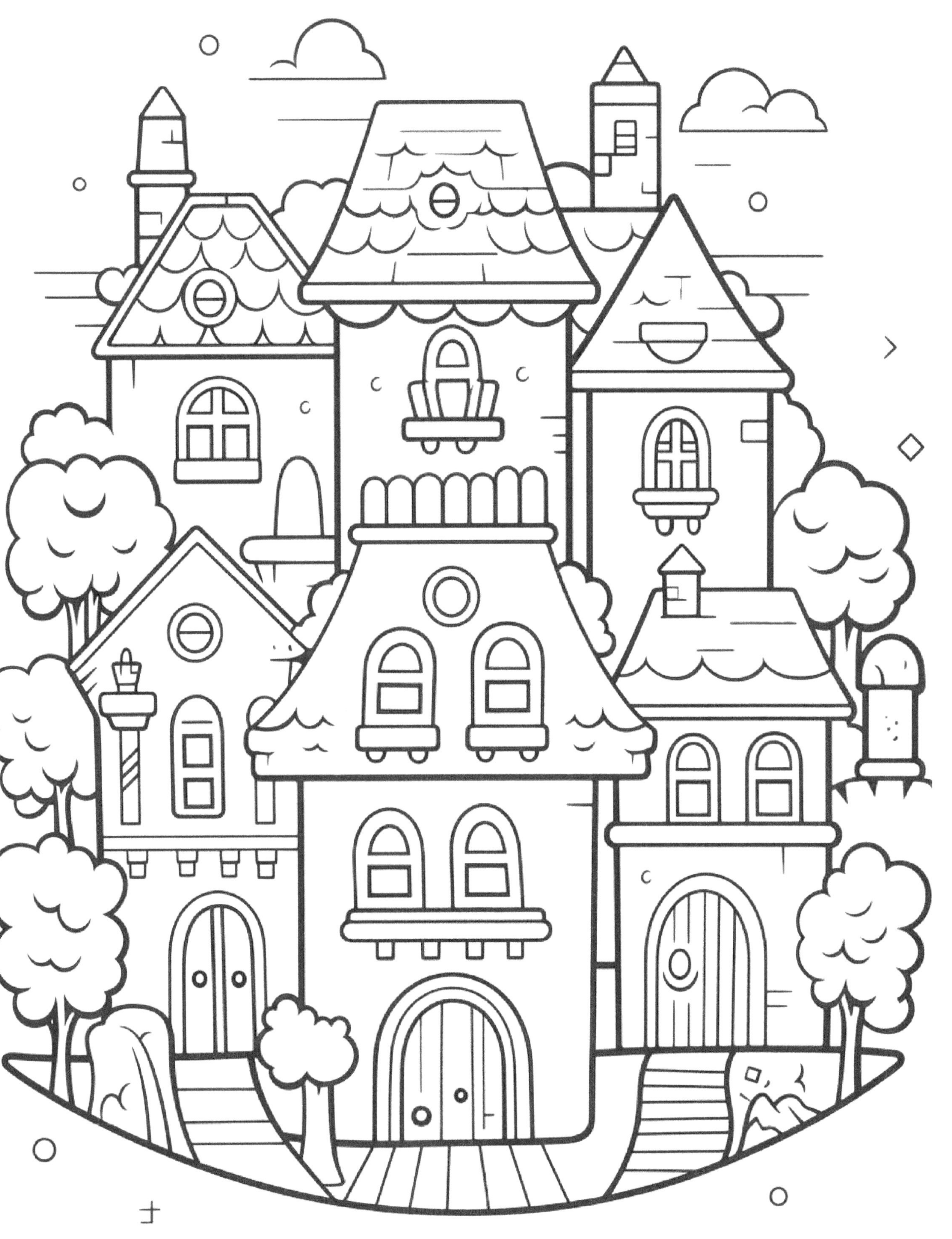

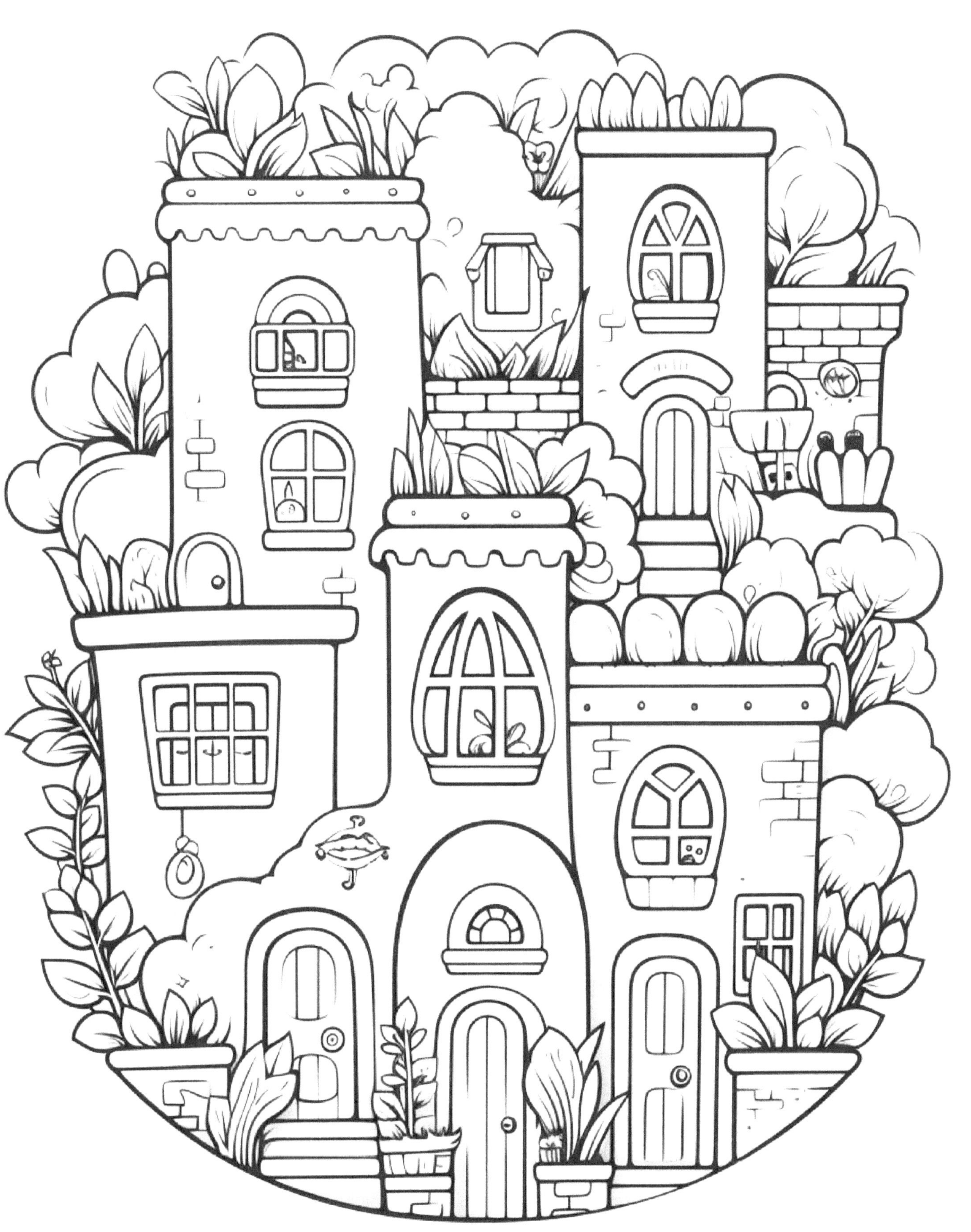

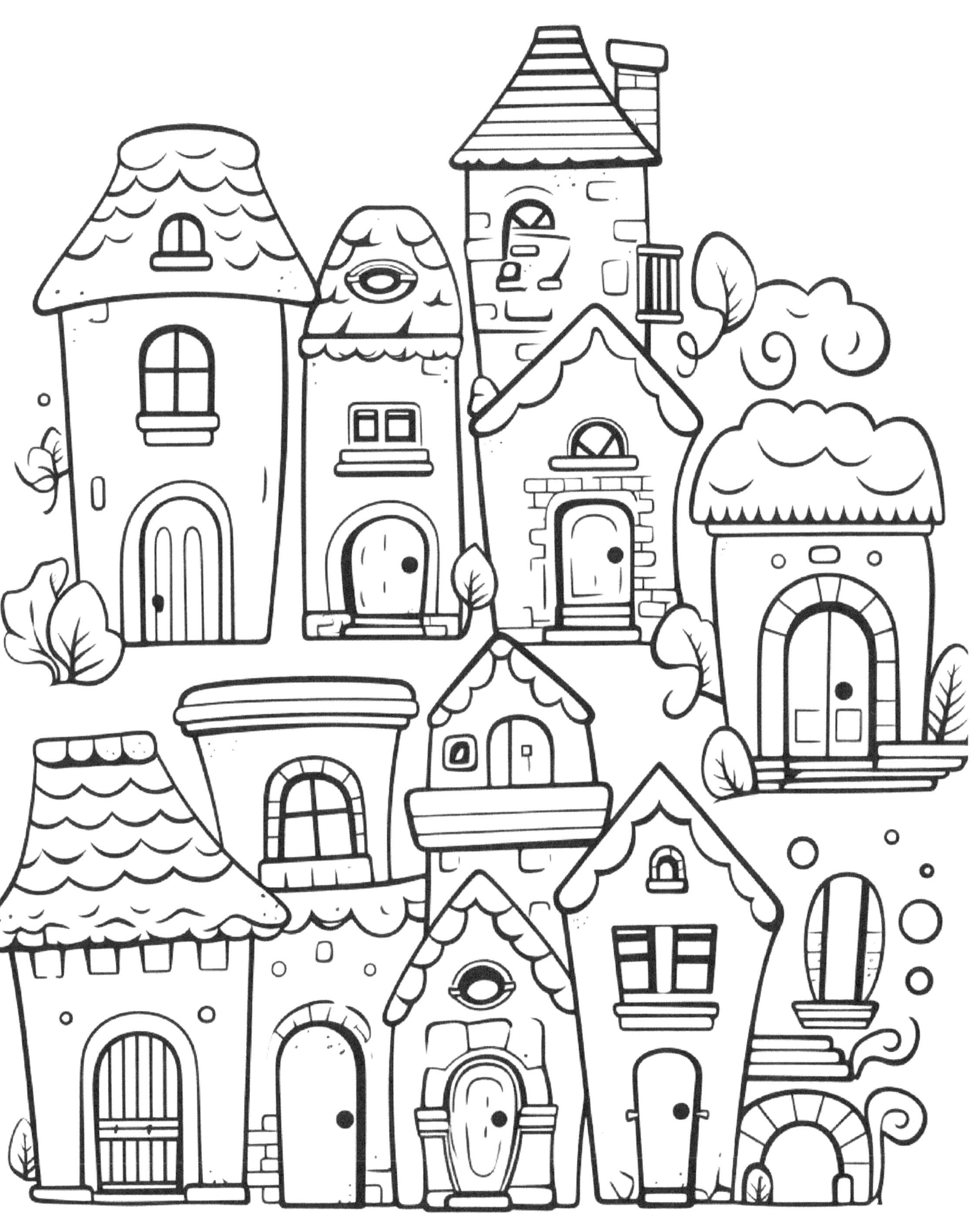

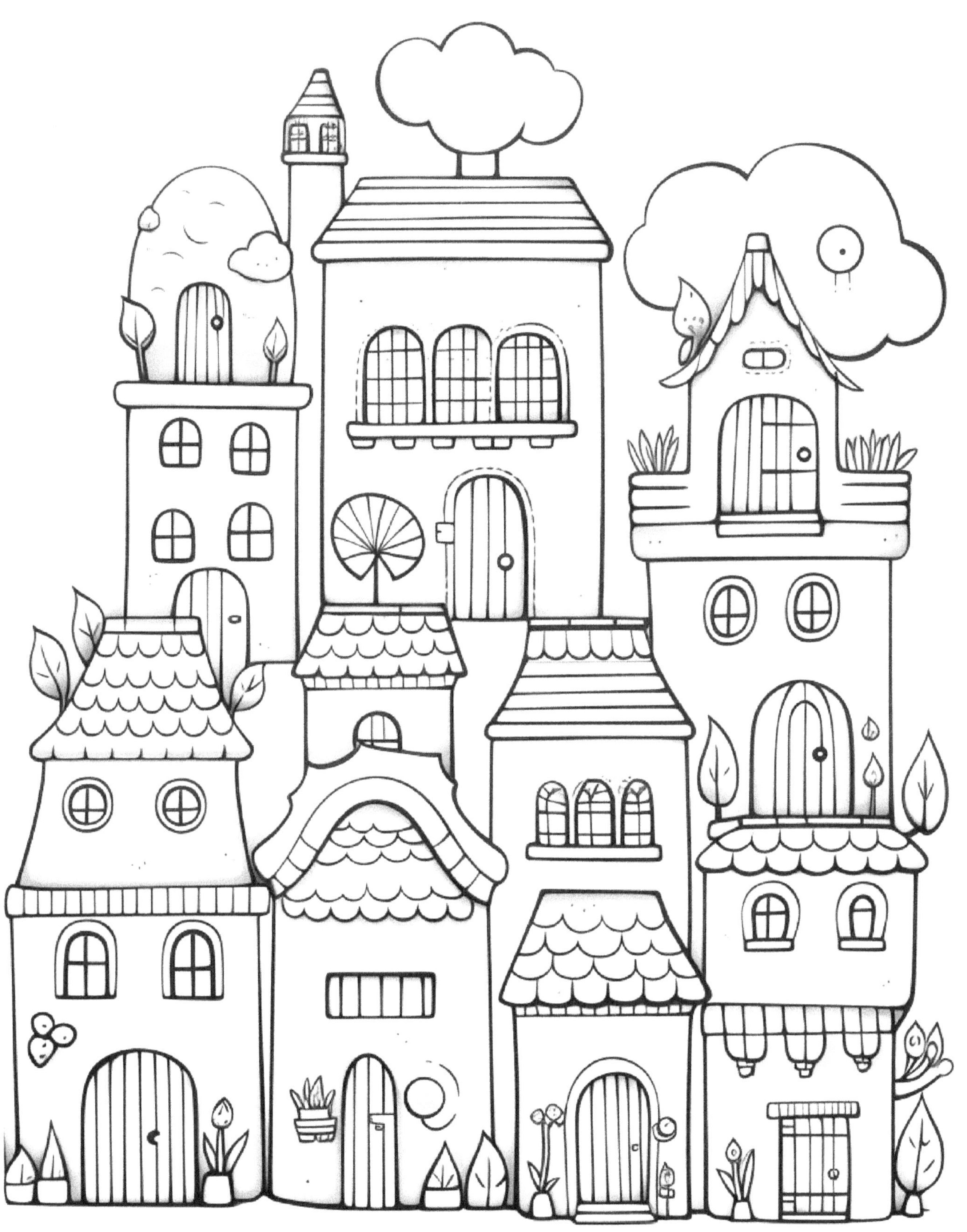

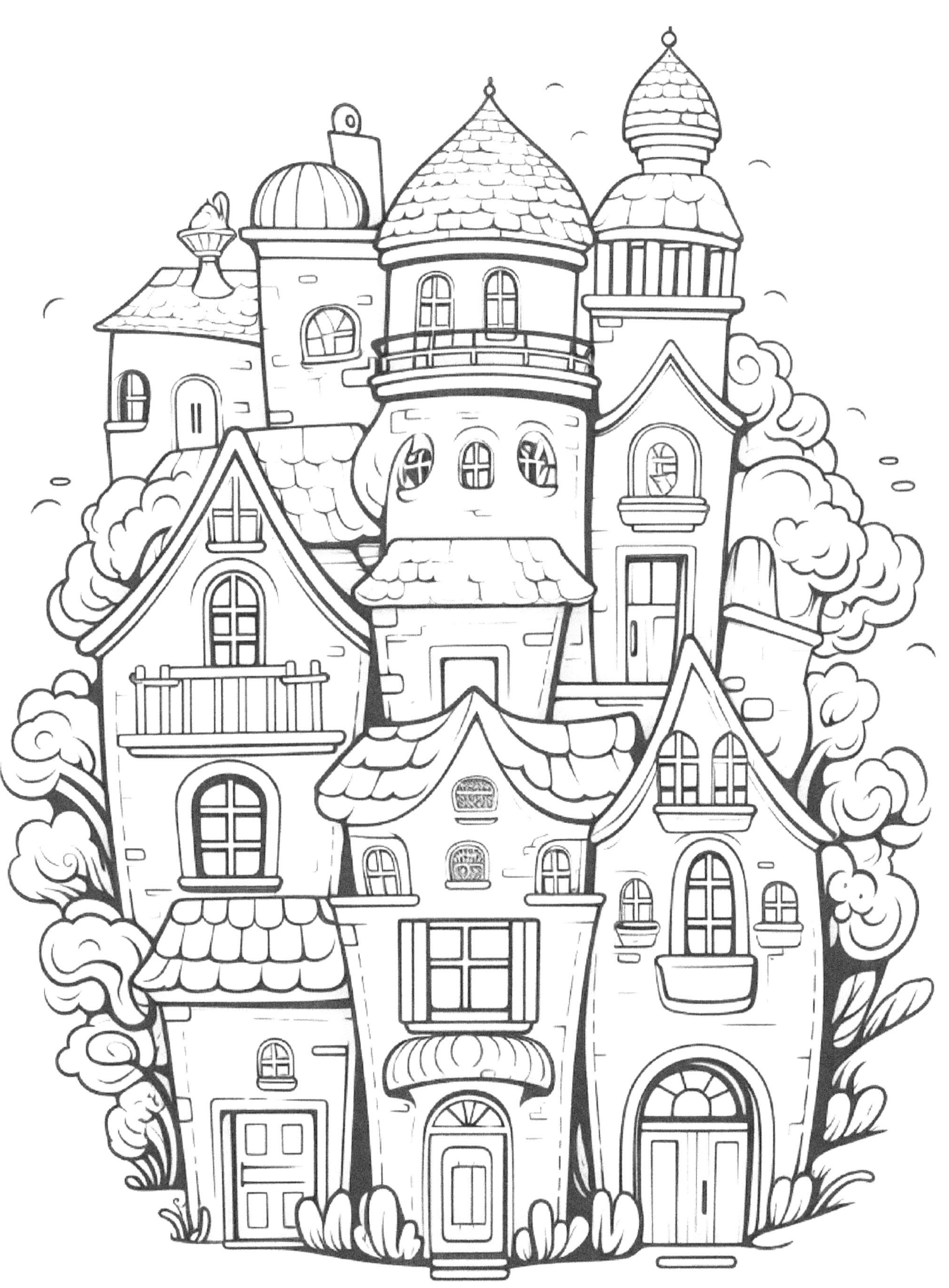